D0396934

ATTRACTER, ENGAGER

Art of the RAINMAKER

ATTRACTER, ENGAGER

Art of the RAINMAKER

The Message, Questions and Insights
that Attract and Engage Clients

BILL WHITLEY

For information about this title or to order other books and/or
electronic media, contact the publisher:
Berkeley Press
214 West Tremont Avenue
Charlotte, NC 28203
www.billwhitley.com
704-996-2800

ISBN: 978-0-9818199-0-7
Printed in the United States of America
Book and cover design by: 1106 Design
Humorous illustrations by: Vlad Kolarov, www.etoonz.com

CONTENTS

ACKNOWLEDGMENTS:

So many people have helped me along my journey; here are eight people who deserve special thanks:

- Jack Prim, my sales manager at Broadway & Seymour (now Jack Henry & Associates) who taught me how to sell.

- Jeffrey Gitomer, a brilliant professional speaker and prolific author who allowed me to travel with him for a year and gave me the opportunity to deliver my first professional presentations.

- Tim Sanders, author of *Love is the Killer App*, who taught me how to collect and share knowledge.

- Norm Trainor, CEO of The Covenant Group, who helped me shape these ideas for advisors and gave me a platform to share them.

- Dr. Tom Hill, author of *Living at the Summit,* who encouraged me to write a book and introduced me to important strategic partners.

- Doug Stevenson, who gave me new insights for developing and delivering stories using his Story Theater Method.

- Laurie Reid, my brilliant editor who made this book make sense.

- My wonderful wife LeeAnne, who survived the Off Field Landing and continues to help and encourage me every day.

Introduction

WHY THIS BOOK?

Would you like more clients? ... would you like deeper relationships that would allow you to do more business with the clients you already have? If so, this book is for you.

"Clients...clients..."

Who should read it?

This book is for advisors, wealth managers, accountants, attorneys, consultants and entrepreneurs. In short, this book is for anybody who makes money by advising clients. Consultative sales professionals will recognize its value, but it is written mainly for people who never intended to be in sales. This book is for people who do what they do because they love doing it and realize that they will never thrive until they attract more clients and grow their business.

If this sounds like you, keep reading. You are about to learn how to create the message, questions and insights that will attract, engage and keep clients loyal ... forever.

On these pages you will find a practical approach to implementing proven ideas without being pushy and without using coercive sales tactics. If you implement these ideas your clients will appreciate you more. As you become more valuable to your clients, you will not only grow your business, you will enjoy it that much more.

Here's to more clients, deeper professional relationships and having more fun at what you do. Cheers!

CONFESSIONS OF A RAINMAKER

M y career started with Wachovia Bank in the Wealth Management Group, but my passion has always been technology and business development. That's what lead me to Broadway & Seymour, a small, rapidly growing technology company that developed software for community banks. For me, it was a wonderful emersion program in technology and sales. I thrived in this environment and within five years became the top salesperson. It was at Broadway & Seymour that I learned to sell but it was my ability to create powerful presentations that propelled me to the top sales position.

I was following my passion when I founded my first company, The Whitley Group, where we developed interactive sales presentations, touch screen kiosks and multi-media training programs. It was during these years that I discovered my gift: the gift of simplicity.

I had the ability to make complex topics simple, visual and easy to understand. Over the next eight years The

"It all comes down to that.."

Whitley Group developed hundreds of sales presentations and training programs. I traveled worldwide working for companies such as IBM, EDS, Ford, AT&T, Apple Computer and Kobe Steel.

We developed presentations that could be shown on laptops to small groups and we developed sophisticated theatrical presentations for trade shows that were played on big screens to thousands of people. No matter how large or small the presentation, our clients hired us for the same reasons: they wanted us to make their complex topics simple, visual and easy to understand. They wanted a message that could be delivered consistently and would make their offerings more desirable and compel prospects to buy.

The Whitley Group grew steadily and in our eighth year we were acquired by iXL, a large internet firm that went public in 1999. We were very lucky to be in the right place at the right time but my journey was not nearly over.

I picked up where The Whitley Group left off and co-founded Mindblazer, a company that created online education-based marketing videos. At Mindblazer I discovered a second gift: the gift of corporate storytelling. I learned how to craft a story that creates a powerful and indelible message; a message that's easy to understand and easy to remember. After selling Mindblazer, I started The Bill Whitley Company, www.billwhitley.com, and launched my career as a professional speaker, author and sales messaging consultant.

I share my background with you simply to let you know that I have walked a mile in your moccasins. In my early years I worked hard to make quota and in running my businesses I have worked hard to attract new clients. Throughout it all, I have worn two hats: that of the creative director as well as the rainmaker. Straddling these two worlds is something that brings me great joy and a unique perspective.

As the creative director I constantly study creativity. I focus on how to develop my personal creativity and how to harness group creativity for business gain. I have learned how to create the insights, ideas and advice that prospects crave. And as the rainmaker I have learned how to use these ideas to attract and engage clients.

Some people follow their passion with reckless abandon. For better or for worse, I'm one of those people. For more than twenty years I have made a living as a storyteller. Not a storyteller in the traditional sense; I am a corporate storyteller.

I help professionals and business owners create messages, conversations, questions and insights that attract and engage clients. And that is what I will share with you in this book.

This book is divided into five parts. The first three sections focus on client attraction, engaging clients and developing authentic enthusiasm. The fourth section addresses methods to magnify your presence and the fifth section provides tools and strategies that you can use to get your team on board. I will share specific techniques and strategies that you can implement immediately to bolster your natural ability in each area.

THE ONE SIMPLE THING

Before we dive into attracting, engaging and creating client insights, I want to share a powerful lesson that I learned years ago. I stumbled upon this lesson quite by accident. You see, the week after I got back from my honeymoon I almost killed my wife.

We were invited to a cocktail party in Richmond, Virginia, in honor of a friend's engagement, a five hour car ride from our home in Charlotte, North Carolina. I had gotten my pilot's license a few months earlier and was able to convince my trusting, new bride LeeAnne, that we could save a lot of travel time by renting the plane that I had taken lessons in and making the journey in a mere ninety minutes.

There was a big headwind the day of our trip and it was taking us longer than expected to get to Richmond. LeeAnne was getting antsy and started looking at her watch. She was worried we would show up late to the party so I pushed that little plane as hard as it would go while Richmond Approach gave me vectors to Hanover County Municipal Airport.

Finally, fifteen long minutes later, the runway came into view. I got ready to enter the landing pattern: downwind, base, final ... nothing to it; this had become old hat for me. While beginning the descent to 800 feet I was daydreaming about being the hot shot that flew us to Richmond in ninety minutes. Then the unthinkable happened. As I turned from downwind to base my engine cut off! For a second I was paralyzed with fear. Could this really be happening? Then I remembered the emergency procedures I had learned in flight school: "Flaps off, find a field." I had heard my instructor say those words countless times during our training flights but now I was going to put them to good use. Take the flaps off so you can glide as long as possible and find a field to land in.

"You're landing where?"

LeeAnne had no idea that we were in jeopardy when I spotted a level farm field off in the distance. I was praying with all of my might when I checked each switch on the control panel to try once again to restart the engine. But, to no avail, we were going down. We continued gliding toward the field getting closer and closer to the rooftops of nearby houses when LeeAnne realized that we were not turning back on the final leg of the landing pattern toward the runway.

"What are you doing?" she asked. I pointed through the windshield to the freshly planted field in front of us and said in the calmest voice I could muster, "We're gonna land in that field." At that point she curled up in a tiny ball and shared some choice words with me. We were so low that we flew under the telephone lines at the edge of the field. We touched down softly and rolled to a stop. Luckily, neither one of us suffered as much as a scrape during the landing and the plane was intact as well.

For a moment I felt pretty good. It was like I was the McGyver of the sky. Then a few seconds later I looked down at the control panel and noticed that something wasn't right. The Mixture Rich/Mixture Lean knob should have been pointing up, but it was pointing straight down. And that's when it hit me. When I turned from downwind to base, the engine didn't turn off by itself, I mistakenly turned it off. Instead of hitting carburetor heat, I hit Mixture Lean and choked the engine. It was a case of human error.

As I sat there feeling like a complete jerk, a wave of pain swept over me. I looked over at my sweet young wife and thought about LeeAnne's parents nurturing this smart, kind, lovely person for twenty-three years. They had kept her safe from the time she was a baby and within one week my mistake, my inexperience, my actions had almost killed her.

Years have since passed. LeeAnne and I now have three children and I have shared this story with many people. Over time I have come to understand that above all else, it was one simple thing that saved us that day. When my engine cut off and I was in the "heat of battle" I knew how to do one simple thing ... **Flaps Off, Find a Field.** My instructor and I had practiced it dozens of times. We would be flying along and he'd reach over and kill the engine and say, "You just lost your engine ... whaddya do?"

My question for you is what's the one simple thing for you?

What's the one simple thing that will help you attract new clients? What's the one simple thing that will help you develop deeper, more intimate client relationships? What's the one simple thing that will allow you to break through and become the trusted advisor you long to be?

I challenge you to find that one simple thing and I promise that this book will give you several great ideas that will help you find it.

WHAT YOU WILL LEARN

In the heat of the "client attraction battle" there are three simple things that will save your life and help you grow your business: your message, your insights and your passion.

Part One —
Client Attraction: Creating Your Message and Your Conversation

Attracting clients starts with your message and how you weave your story into everyday conversation. I call it a **Client Attraction Story:** the one simple message that makes prospective clients want to hire you.

One of the most elusive business skills is the ability to engage a client and educate them about a product or service in a way that creates a natural desire for them to purchase your product. The lion's share of sales and marketing budgets are spent on marketing, branding and lead generation with the intent to open dialogue with prospects. Not nearly as much is invested in teaching people how to attract and engage clients and develop lasting client relationships. If you understand the steps involved in a compelling client attraction story, the rest will fall into place.

Part Two —
Engaging Clients: Creating Questions, Ideas and Insights

Engaging clients requires you to harness your **innovation and creativity.** You will learn how to develop the questions that you will eventually become known for; questions that your clients have never been asked. Questions that, when answered, will enlighten both you and your clients. You know you are on the right track when your clients say, "Wow, I've never been asked that before, that's a good question."

You will learn proven methods to engage your clients in the idea-creation process. As your clients participate in this process, they will have a greater appreciation for the solution you develop together. You will learn how to create better ideas that bring more value to the sale. These ideas will not only be appreciated by your clients, but will differentiate you from every competitor.

Part Three —
Becoming the Trusted Advisor: Creating Passion for What You Do

Part Three of this book deals with the most important part of your success: your deep belief in what you do. When you believe in what you do, you naturally develop something

I call **Authentic Enthusiasm.** It is elusive but when developed properly your client attraction story, your conversation, your questions and your insights will naturally instill Authentic Enthusiasm into all of your communication.

Your Authentic Enthusiasm speaks louder than words. Once you have developed Authentic Enthusiasm you're no longer selling — you're helping, and that is the most powerful position in selling. When you shift from selling to helping you become a client advocate. You become a trusted advisor.

As you become your clients' trusted advisor, five things will naturally occur:

1. You will make more sales

2. You will deliver more value

3. You will create loyal clients

4. You will receive more introductions

5. You will enjoy your job more

Part Four —
Expanding Your Presence and Extending Your Sphere of Influence

Once you have mastered attracting and engaging, Part Four will show you how to magnify your presence and attract even more clients. You will learn how to develop your thought leadership, how to create a referral-rich environment and how to make your message available over the Internet with a video story package.

Part Five —
Final Thoughts

Part Five will help you harness what you have learned by sharing it with your team. This section covers coaching employees and creating a visual representation of your vision that is easy to understand and remember. This section is designed to show you how to help your team to help you. Let's get started!

Part One

Client Attraction: Creating Your Message and Your Conversation

I t all begins with a story ... your Client Attraction Story. You will learn the mechanics of stories and a step-by-step approach for developing your Client Attraction Story a bit later, but first let me share an example of a great Client Attraction Story.

I was recently leading a seminar on "The Art of Attracting and Engaging Clients" for 250 insurance agents. I shared the five parts of a story and the five powers of a story. Then we did an interactive exercise where I asked each participant to work on their Client Attraction Story. At the end of the exercise I made a deal with the audience, "If two or three people will share their story with the group I will listen, take notes, digest your story and I'll share with you exactly how I'd tell your story if I sold for you." My first volunteer was Mike who shared the story on the following page.

A Client Attraction Story

" I have a client who is a college professor. He's a smart guy. He's a nice guy. One day he was driving home from work and it started to rain. You know how when it starts to rain people will run and try to get out of the rain? Well, he lives in a cute little college town. The main street has a row of brick storefronts and striped awnings. It started to rain and a guy tried to run across the street to get under an awning and get out of the rain ... and my college professor didn't see him ... and he hit him with his car.

"$900,000 later, the last medical bill was paid.

"Fortunately, one year before the accident my professor bought a $1,000,000 personal umbrella policy from me. There's not a day that goes by that he doesn't call me and thank me for selling him that policy.

"By the way, if he hadn't bought the policy, a typical chain of events would have occurred. First he would have exhausted all his savings to pay that guys medical bills, then he would have gone into debt, then he would have declared bankruptcy. But because he bought the policy, there was no financial impact."

As Mike told the story I was grinning from ear to ear. What a powerful story. When Mike finished I looked out at the agents in the room and said, "You don't have to know how to sell personal umbrella insurance, you just have to know how to tell that one story."

Once mastered, stories like this become your most valuable assets. They become your strongest client attraction tools. I suggested that each of the agents tell that story to every member of their team. Have each team member tell it back once the story is learned.

The story has to be mastered in order to become an effective sales tool. It has to be something that you can instantly recall and deliver flawlessly. Just like **Flaps Off, Find a Field,** you should be able to instantly recall and tell the story. Of course, the more you tell your story the more accomplished you will become.

Five Parts of a Great Story

Everyone loves a great story. That's why we enjoy movies, books and TV. The classic story format has five main parts. Think back to the stories and fairy tales you were told as a child. When your parents or grandparents read you a bedtime story I'm sure they sounded something like this:

1. Once upon a time there was a hero

2. Who had a reason to go on a journey

3. Where he/she/it met a huge challenge

4. To which there was a hero-inspired way out

5. And they all lived happily ever after

Client Attraction Stories have the same five key parts. Let's take a look:

1. *Once upon a time there was a hero...*
   In a Client Attraction Story your client is always the hero. This is where you introduce your client

and provide a little information about their situation. Mike did this beautifully with his Client Attraction Story about the personal umbrella policy when he said, "I have a client who is a college professor. He's a smart guy. He's a nice guy." With that short description we now have an understanding of the hero's background, and the context for the story is set.

2. *Who had a reason to go on a journey...*
   Remember the fairy tale starts with, "Once upon a time there was a hero who had reason to go on a journey." In a Client Attraction Story, the journey is simply the goal the client wants to achieve. It's the quest — that one illusive thing they are trying to achieve. In the case of the college professor it was his desire to financially protect himself from the unforeseen future.

3. *Where he met a huge challenge...*
   The client runs into an obstacle. No matter how hard he tries, something always holds him back. Hitting the pedestrian during the rain storm was something the college professor could not have foreseen.

4. *To which there was a hero-inspired way out...*
   With your help the client overcomes the obstacle. This is the most important part of the story. Identify what steps the client took to overcome the obstacle

and how you helped in the process. This is where the learning takes place. The obstacle would have been insurmountable had the college professor not bought that policy suggested by his agent.

5. *And he lives happily ever after...*
Thanks to the solution you helped the client implement, his life changes for the better. It usually involves increased revenue, increased profit or an efficiency gain. In the case of the college professor, it saved him from financial ruin.

Five Powers 3 of a Story

Stories elicit emotional responses, capturing our hearts and our imaginations. People might not remember statistics but they will remember a good story. Using stories to sell your products and services is a powerful form of persuasion.

A well-crafted story will give you powers if you use them to your advantage:

1. Stories Entertain — The Power to Attract and Hold Attention

2. Stories are Rich with Detail — The Power to Establish Instant Credibility

3. Stories Create Context — The Power to Explain What Really Happened

4. Stories Create a Vicarious Experience — The Power to Deliver Your Message

5. Stories are Easy to Remember and Retell — The Power of Consistency

One: Stories Entertain — The Power to Attract and Hold Attention

If you think engaging and persuading a business audience is tough, try holding the attention of a bunch of six year olds. A few weeks ago, I was at an Indian Guides meeting with my six-year-old son and eleven of his squirmiest friends. As you might imagine there was a lot of laughing and joking and not very much listening going on. My job was to tell the boys a story. As our tribe's "sand painter" I was asked to tell a story with unique and profound meaning that would help the boys along their journey in life. Wow. Now that's a tall order. Determined to succeed, I bought Bill Bennett's *Book of Virtues* and told a story about a king who was returning from a hunting trip. As the king headed home with his trusty falcon, he stopped to dip his cup into a small stream to get a drink. Before he could bring his cup to his mouth his falcon swooped down and knocked the cup away. He tried again, and again his falcon knocked the cup away. The third time the falcon flew down to knock the cup away the enraged king drew his sword and killed the bird.

Later, as his falcon lay dead on the ground, the king realized that the stream he was trying to drink from had been poisoned. His faithful hunting companion had been trying to save his life. Of course the king felt terrible and as he stood there, on that spot, at that moment, the king vowed he would never again make a decision that was motivated by anger.

As I told the story (in much greater detail to the boys), I realized that for the first time during our one hour meeting the room was completely quiet. Every boy was riveted by the story. I had captured their attention; my audience was engaged and the message was delivered.

Two: Stories are Rich with Detail — The Power to Establish Instant Credibility

As you read my story earlier about almost killing my wife and landing in the freshly planted soybean field, was there any doubt that I am a pilot — although maybe not a good pilot? To establish credibility, I provided a lot of detail and used pilot lingo such as, "Richmond Approach gave me vectors to Hanover County Municipal Airport. When I saw the runway I dropped down to 800 feet, entered the landing pattern and put on one notch of flaps, as I turned base I put on a second notch of flaps." When I tell that story no one doubts that I am a private pilot (or at least *was* a private pilot). The language in my story establishes instant credibility with my audience; they have no doubt that I know what I'm talking about. If only I could fly as well as I can tell that story.

Three: Stories Create Context — The Power to Explain What Really Happened

I have a client who is a general agent with the Northwestern Mutual Financial Network whose primary job is to recruit insurance agents. There are two types of candidates: early career changers and later career changers. When talking with later career changers my client often tells this story:

"Joe is one of my top agents. He's ranked in the top one percent of all Northwestern agents for both insurance and investments. Joe graduated from college in 1988 with a degree in finance. After he passed the Series 7 he went to work for a financial planning company and stayed with them for nine years.

"He was doing well but he eventually became frustrated that his owners wouldn't share ownership. Deep inside Joe had an entrepreneurial spirit and wanted to control his destiny. After several unsuccessful attempts to negotiate an ownership position, he decided to make a change.

"He looked at all the big investment firms. During his evaluation phase, a friend of his told him he should consider Northwestern. At first he dismissed us because he thought of us as an insurance company and he was more comfortable with investments, but he agreed to at least take a look.

"As part of his due diligence Joe met with us and caught on to the vision of the Northwestern Financial Network. He realized that we are much more than an insurance company. But more importantly he was impressed with our culture. Specifically he liked that we:

- Are more family oriented
- Are more team oriented
- Always try to do the right thing for the client
- Have a proven strategy for acquiring new clients

"When he did his final analysis he realized we were a perfect fit. He could plug his financial planning and investment knowledge into our proven client acquisition strategy and client-oriented culture and he could begin building his own business. He also liked that we had solid ways to keep him on track and he could build a business that he owns — a business he can eventually pass on to his children."

This story is a great example of the power of context. My client knows that other seasoned financial advisors may have the same concerns that Joe had — "You guys are just an insurance company and I'm an investment guy." By telling this story, it's easy to understand Joe's concerns, his selection process and how he combined what he knew with Northwestern's strengths to become a top player.

The power of context gives you the ability to create desire as well as the ability to head off potential objections before they ever come up.

Four: Stories Create a Vicarious Experience — The Power to Deliver Your Message

The best teacher is an experience, but in most cases you can't offer your prospect an experience so a vicarious experience is the next best thing. Stories are an easy way to convey a vicarious experience. Your client will have a better appreciation and understanding of your products and services if they can live it vicariously through your story.

In the book *Influencer... The Power to Change Anything*, authors Patterson, Grenny, Maxfield, McMillan and Switzler share a great example of a vicarious experience. One of the master influencers the authors study is psychologist Dr. Albert Bandura. To prove the power of a vicarious experience Dr. Bandura ran an ad in the *Palo Alto News* asking anyone with a paralyzing fear of snakes to come to the psychology department to be cured. Over one hundred people showed up. Some of the people had such a tremendous fear that they were practically shut-ins, unable to venture out of the house because of their snake phobia.

Dr. Bandura did not lecture the participants. No amount of words can convince someone to give up an irrational fear. Instead he used a much more powerful technique. He let the group watch someone handle a snake. This is known as a *vicarious experience*. Dr. Bandura asked participants to watch through a doorway as a therapist walked into a room where a terrarium housed a five-foot snake. The therapist opened the terrarium, petted the snake, then picked up the snake and put it on his lap. The participants viewing from behind the window saw that the therapist was safe and the snake seemed harmless. Then Dr. Bandura asked each participant to do the same thing. Some requested protective gear such as hockey goalie gloves, a baseball catcher's chest protector and a sturdy mask. Donning the protective gear, each participant entered the room and stood near the terrarium. Gradually, they worked up the nerve to remove the lid. Later the participants touched the snake and finally sat with the snake draped over their lap. The entire process took only three hours and each participant was completely cured.

Dr. Bandura and his team had discovered something profound. First, if you want people to change their behavior, drop verbal persuasion and come up with innovative ways to create personal experiences. Second, when you can't take everyone on a field trip, create vicarious experiences.

You can change how people view your products and services by sharing vibrant and credible stories. Told well, these vicariously-created events approximate the gold standard of change: real experience.

Five: Stories are Easy to Remember and Retell — The Power of Consistency

I helped form an early stage venture fund several years ago. Over a three-year period we listened to over one hundred investor presentations. The best presentation I heard was given by a company called FloLogic. Instead of taking the typical approach of talking about their management team and presenting charts showing their market domination, the FloLogic principals designed their presentation around this compelling story:

A family finishes loading their car, backs down the driveway and heads out of town. Their much-anticipated vacation is finally here. They will be gone for nine glorious, fun-filled days. Their home is fairly new with a design that locates the washing machine and dryer on the second floor. Ten minutes after the happy family pulls out of the driveway the hose to their washing machine ruptures. Water gushes from the ruptured hose at the rate of six gallons per minute. Over the course of nine days more than 76,000 gallons of water floods their home.

The well-rested family returns home the following Sunday. When they open the door they enter a disaster area. The ceiling has collapsed, the first-floor walls are saturated and the carpeting, furniture, memorabilia, antiques and electronics are completely destroyed.

The family is forced to move into an extended-stay motel for three months while their home is rebuilt and refurnished. The insurance company's financial loss and the family's personal loss are enormous.

Is this story far-fetched? Not according to industry research that reports that nearly 50,000 claims are filed annually for damage caused by ruptured washing machine hoses.

Then the presenter shared how to rewrite the story's end:

> FloLogic is like a circuit breaker for your water pipes. It knows how much water you normally use. It also has "home" and "away" modes so that the second it detects abnormal water use, it shuts off the water supply. In the rewrite, when the family returns home the house is exactly as they remembered it.

Unlike most investor presentations, FloLogic built its presentation around a story. They made their product and the need for it easy to understand, but they also made it easy for us to explain their concept to others. Years later I still tell the FloLogic story verbatim. Stories are not only easy to understand and remember, but easy to repeat. This is critical when selling, because sometimes you're not talking to the person who writes the check. If you explain what you do with a good Client Attraction Story, I guarantee it's more likely that whomever you speak with will be able to convey what you do to the person who writes the check.

My Personal Client Attraction Story

Before you begin working on developing your story let me share my Client Attraction Story with you. I launched The Bill Whitley Company in the summer of 2007 and am enjoying life as a professional speaker. Public speaking has always been a passion of mine. After selling my second company I worked selling online training and filled in as a professional speaker when needed. I knew it was time to head out on my own and form my own speaking business when I had a story — a Client Attraction Story.

❖ ❖ ❖

I was hired by a large insurance company to go to Los Angeles and deliver my half-day seminar, "The Art of Attracting and Engaging Clients" to 250 agents. They told me a typical agent could write 15 to 20 auto policies per month, but the best agents write 60 to 70 per month. "Your job," they said, "is to help the typical agent move up the ladder. These agents may never write 60 to 70 policies a month, but if you can get them to 30 a month, that would be a huge victory."

I told them I would be delighted to teach the seminar but before I did so, I would like to interview the top ten agents. I wanted to find out what made them so effective. I spent well over an hour with many of my interviewees. By the end of the interviews I was amazed with what I had learned. I called my key contact at the company and said, "Jim, I'm so excited about what I learned in these interviews that I have decided to change the name of my seminar to 'Eight Secrets of the Top Performing Agents.' Would you like to hear secret number one?" The answer, of course, was yes and I dove right in. "Secret number one is that early in the conversation, the top agents position themselves as risk managers." Now you might not be impressed with that secret, but let me explain exactly what these agents do.

"When they receive a request for an auto insurance quote, most agents will reply, 'Sure I'd be delighted to help with that. What kind of car do you have?' They provide the quote without adding any other value: they are quoters.

"The top agents take a totally different approach. When asked for an auto insurance quote they respond with, 'I'd be delighted to help you, let me ask a few questions.' Question number one is, 'So ... how did you hear about us?' and thus begins the task of gathering information that will enable them to become more than just a quoter. Question two, 'How many cars do you own?' Yes, the client owns two cars: his and his wife's. Question three, 'Do you and your wife own a home?' Yes, the client owns a home.

"And finally the agent asks, 'Do you and your wife have investments?' At which point, some callers will say, 'You know what? I'm really just looking to save a little money on car insurance; I'm not interested in the other stuff.'"

All of the agents I interviewed responded differently, but the gist of what they said was, "If the only thing you want is cheap auto insurance, I guarantee you can get it cheaper somewhere else. But I can tell you and your wife are successful and have accumulated some wealth. If you'd like me to take a look at what you own and recommend the most effective way to protect your assets, then I am your guy. And by the way, if I write multiple lines for you covering your cars, your home and include a personal umbrella policy, I can offer you a significant multi-line discount. So ultimately, I *will* save you money on auto insurance. But you need to think of me as your risk manager. Is that of interest to you?"

At the end of my seminar, one of guys who hired me walked up and said, "I can't believe how easy your program is to follow, understand and execute." The day after the seminar, I received a call from Jim, who said, "You will not believe this, but I'm getting calls from agents saying that they are no longer just quoting. They are now asking better questions; they're positioning themselves as risk managers and they are not only closing more autos, they are selling more lines per client!" My client was thrilled.

❖ ❖ ❖

I have told that story hundreds of times. It is my Client Attraction Story and I believe it has great power. A few months ago I called a business acquaintance who is a national sales manager responsible for 250 sales reps who sell technology to banks. It was November when I called and I wanted to pitch him on hiring me to speak at his company's national sales meeting in July. I left a message saying, "Stan, this is Bill Whitley. I just developed a seminar for a large insurance company and it was a huge success. When you hear about it I think you might want me to do the same thing for you. Give me a call when you have a chance and I'll tell you about it."

A few days later he called and I shared my Client Attraction Story with him. It took me about six minutes to tell my story. Stan listened and when I was done he said, "Let me get this straight: you interviewed their top agents, looked for commonality and then synthesized their best practices. Then you developed a client engagement process and a sales message and taught the rest of their agents how to attract and engage clients." I agreed; that is exactly what happened. I'll never forget Stan's reply, "Bill, there is no sales manager in America that wouldn't want that. To be honest with you, I don't want to wait until July. I've got two regional sales meetings in January, one in Dallas and one in Orlando. We already have the agenda set, but I don't think we have signed any contracts. I'll call you back in a couple of days." Two days later Stan called, "You're in."

"If you know how to open, you don't have to close"

That is the power of a good Client Attraction Story. It took six minutes for me to tell my story and in that time Stan understood the value that I brought and envisioned the results that I could help him achieve. But before he experienced his own positive results he experienced the results vicariously by listening to my story. And a vicarious experience is the next best thing to an actual experience. Your stories have the power to create a vicarious experience.

Now it's your turn. Before you select a story to develop I want you to think about your ideal client. In other words, if all of your clients could be just like one client, what would that client be like? It's important to know this before you start on your story because your story will attract clients similar to the one in your story.

"New clients ahead, Sir!"

Your story will evolve so don't get hung up on finding the perfect story. But you need a story that aims your client attraction efforts in the right direction. So pick a story that represents the clients you want to attract. Once the story is completed, jump in and start using it. Just like a book that is never read, a story that is never told has no value. To find your ideal story start by answering the questions in the next section.

Now it's **5**Your Turn...
Client Attraction Story Activities

What is the biggest impact any of your ideal clients
have had?

1.	
2.	
3.	
4.	
5.	

What are your ideal client's biggest challenges?

1.	
2.	
3.	
4.	
5.	

What are the most valuable things you have created for your ideal clients?

1.	
2.	
3.	
4.	
5.	

Take a look at the answers above. Does one specific "ideal client" story come to mind? Develop that story with the exercise below.

Activity: Creating Your Client Attraction Story

Take some time now to begin developing your own Client Attraction Story.

1. Introduce the client (hero) and give a little background

2. Begin the journey; define the goal or the task to be accomplished

3. Describe the obstacle that the client encounters

4. Explain how, with your help, the client overcomes the obstacle

5. State the moral of the story: what the client learned

1. Client background ...

2. Client wanted to achieve ...

3. Something got in the way ...

4. How you helped ...

5. The results ...

Story  Themes

N ow that you have created a powerful Client Attraction Story, you will use it to grow your business. I have told my Client Attraction Story to many people over the years. Regardless of the prospective client's business background, my one story always works for me.

Some people find that it works better if they have more than one Client Attraction Story in their arsenal. Having several stories memorized, perfected and at their fingertips ensures that they have a story to fit any circumstance that they encounter.

Here are some of the common themes you may wish to consider.

Six themes behind the Client Attraction Stories:

1. Why Me?: Focus on integrity, commitment and follow-through

2. Growth: Focus on increased revenue and market share

3. Efficiency: Focus on increased profit and saving time and money

4. Buy Right: Focus on making the right decision and offering good advice

5. Recruiting: Focus on why you work here, more income, more equity and more fulfillment

6. Protection: Focus on keeping me, my assets and my income safe

Think of the themes as "handles" that you can use to select the right story for the right occasion. If you're talking with someone who wants to grow his business, use a growth story.

Sample Client Attraction Stories

Now that you understand the five parts of a good story, the five powers of a good story and have a feel for the different themes of a good Client Attraction Story, take a few minutes to read and experience some of the stories I've been told over the years. They may help you create your Client Attraction Stories.

Theme One — Why Me?: Focus on integrity, commitment and follow-though

Here's an example from a client who is a leading provider of technology for banks and credit unions. This story does a great job of highlighting the importance of integrity, commitment and follow-through: doing what you said you would do.

Background

Our philosophy is simply "Do the right thing, do whatever it takes."

Four and-a-half years ago we signed a start-up bank that is located an hour west of Philadelphia. Their CEO is a sharp guy and in less than five years they have already grown to $200 million and opened three branches.

Journey

They didn't want to tie up a lot of capital when it came to operations, so they outsourced everything to us — even their check processing.

Challenge

They looked at all the usual suspects before they opened their doors. They liked our system the best but there was one major problem: we had no local item processing center that could service them. We wanted their business, so as part of the deal, we committed to build an item processing center that would serve their bank. Unfortunately, we made a mistake. We built the center closer to New York and it should have been closer to Philadelphia. The CEO was disappointed with our choice of location.

Solution

Our philosophy is to do the right thing; do whatever it takes. So we set up an interim solution to handle his checks while we built a center closer to Philadelphia that could handle his items for the long term.

Results

We kept our promise and made good on our commitments. They are now happy customers and I'm sure they will do business with us for a long time to come.

Ask the Question

So how about you? Is having a partner that does the right thing and does whatever it takes to get it right important to you? As you make this investment, I challenge you to find the right partner — a partner that will stand behind their commitments and do the right thing.

❖ ❖ ❖

Here's another example of commitment and follow-through. This story comes from a large insurance company:

Background

One of my clients is a newly married couple. He works for a food distribution company and she works at the YMCA.

Journey

They had just purchased their first home. After making this investment they decided to buy life insurance to make sure they could keep their home even if something happened to either one of them.

Challenge

Unfortunately, he was overweight and has some medical issues so he was denied coverage.

Solution

I was determined to make sure that they get the coverage they needed, so I went to bat for him and got him a table rating and was able to get him covered.

Results

Over the years my client's health deteriorated and he died at age 42.

When I presented his wife a check for $200,000 she hugged me and thanked me and said, "I can't tell you how much I appreciate the fact that you went to bat for my husband. Thanks to you I can keep our house."

Ask the Question

Is having an insurance agent who will go to bat for you important? As you make this investment, I challenge you to find an agent who cares about your financial security.

✤ ✤ ✤

This example of a commitment and follow-through story is from an online mortgage banking company:

Background

I was working with a married couple who were expecting their first baby.

Journey

Their goal was to buy a home and move in before the baby was born.

Challenge

As first-time, low-income homebuyers they were bombarded with information — not only from loan officers, but from every family member and friend as well. They were overwhelmed and didn't know what to do.

Solution

When I started working with them I could sense their confusion and frustration. They didn't have much money and the loans that they were offered were not very appealing. As I listened to their needs and studied their options I realized they were the perfect candidates for a "My Community" loan. It's a good solution for low-income families with higher debt.

Results

They got the loan and were in the house one month before their baby was born. I was the only loan officer who took the time to evaluate their situation and offer them this mortgage which was by far the best price and best deal.

Ask the Question

Are you inundated and overwhelmed with loan information? Do you want an experienced mortgage advisor to help you wade through all the information and get the best product at the best price?

Theme 2 — Growth: Focus on increased revenue and market share

This story, from a client that provides technology to banks and credit unions, demonstrates how to help a customer increase market share.

"The Robin Hood of the banking world"

Background

One of the things I like most about my job is helping small banks take business away from big banks. I feel like the Robin Hood of the banking world. One of my clients is the executive vice president of an $800 million bank in Virginia.

Journey

My client was looking for ways to grow deposits and expand the bank's commercial market.

Challenge

Historically they had a hard time picking up commercial accounts because, unlike larger regional banks, they don't have as many branches in all the convenient locations.

Solution

After installing Merchant Capture (our technology system), everything changed for my client. Geography was no longer an issue as items can be captured, transmitted and handled electronically. No need to visit the branch — just scan the checks and press "send".

Results

Within one year of installing Merchant Capture their deposits grew by $25 million and they opened 400 new commercial accounts. They have been so successful my client feels like the entire eastern seaboard is now his marketplace.

Ask the Question

So how about you? Are you interested in increasing market share and picking up more commercial accounts?

Theme Three — Efficiency: Focus on increased profit and saving time and money

This story comes to us from a provider of point-of-sale terminals for restaurants. It shows how they helped their clients increase efficiency, improve service and improve profit:

Background

One of my clients owns a small chain of four restaurants in Arizona. Her restaurants have a hip, Zen feel and serve high quality, hot food quickly. My client is in her mid-forties and she was terrified of computers.

Journey

Her goal is to grow her chain to over twenty stores in the next four years.

Challenge

She delegated the selection of point-of-sale terminals to her son because she was uncomfortable with computers. Unfortunately, he chose the lowest-priced system and it never performed up to par. To make matters worse, the vendor eventually went out of business. My client needed to make a change, and after being burned she was even more nervous about technology.

Solution

To earn her trust, we offered to install our system in one of her locations at no upfront cost and we agreed that if she didn't like it, she wouldn't owe us a dime. She agreed and we installed our system in one of her locations. The employees at that location were thrilled with the ease of our system.

Results

The system went live on Tuesday, which is historically their slowest day. But because of the speed and efficiency of the new system they set a record — earning thirty percent more revenue than any other location. When my client realized how much more efficient her restaurants could be, she had us install our system in all of her locations.

Ask the Question

So how about you? Are you interested in setting a new record in earnings?

"And that's how in short we will conquer the world!"

❖ ❖ ❖

Here's another great efficiency story from a restaurant technology provider:

Background

One of my clients is a moderate-sized zoo with three concession areas. I was working with their food and beverage manager.

Journey

He wanted a more efficient operation.

Challenge

Unfortunately, they were using standard cash registers which do not provide the information that he needed to make managerial decisions. They didn't have basic information like which food items are the best sellers. Staffing was a challenge as they didn't have data showing which days and times were the busiest. In the remote concession area, if a customer used a credit card, the staff had to run the card to the main concession center, process the transaction and run it back. My client needed some serious help.

Solution

We worked with the zoo to design and install a system with seventeen terminals on one network. They now have:

- Consolidated reporting in all three areas

- A centrally-managed system making it easier to adjust prices and menu items

- Touch-screen application that makes training easier

- Real-time information determining best sellers and busy times

- One remote area with wireless transaction processing for credit cards

"Do the math..."

Results

My client now knows the fifteen busiest days of the year and can plan accordingly. On each of those fifteen days, he says they handle $500 more per terminal. If you do the math: fifteen days × seventeen terminals × $500 is an increase of $127,500 in revenue. Not to mention employees used to give items away rather than deal with the hassle of ringing them up correctly. The zoo is experiencing increased revenue, increased efficiency and touch-screen terminals that makes staff training much easier thanks to the system we installed.

Ask the Question

At the end of his busy season I asked my client what he learned and he said, "If you have the right tools and know how to use them, you can make a lot more money."

Theme Four — Buy Right: Focus on making the right decision and offering good advice

Here's an example of a "good advice" story from my mortgage banking client:

Background

I recently helped a couple named Erica and Anthony. They buy and sell homes. They have great credit, strong income and a low loan-to-value ratio. They are a lender's dream.

Journey

Their goal was to get the lowest interest rate by timing the market.

Problem

Unfortunately, they were passing up homes while waiting for the rate to drop lower and lower.

Solution

As their advisor I was able to get them the best mortgage at the best price. I shared with them that rates are at an all-time low. Then I recommended that they lock in with the free float-down feature which allows them to float down if the rate ever drops again. The bonus was that if rates went up, they are locked in and protected.

Results

As soon as Erica and Anthony understood, they locked in. They got the best rate and the deal closed quickly.

Ask the Question

So what about you? Wouldn't it be smart to lock in now and guarantee that you're protected?

✣ ✣ ✣

This story from a bank technology provider client illustrates the value of buying right the first time:

Background

One of our banks is located in a very affluent area of California, not far from Rodeo Drive. There are lots of businesses within a mile of the bank.

Journey

This bank has an aggressive management team and their goal is to grow quickly. Their target market is commercial businesses and high-net-worth individuals.

Problem

Unfortunately, their core system was holding them back. Three years ago when they did their evaluation, they went with a cheaper system. It looked fine on the surface but they now realize that it doesn't have the level of integration that their clients demand. For example, online banking and cash management are not integrated back to the core so their online clients are always a day behind. They were also frustrated with the level of product support. When they voiced their concerns the answer was always, "Sorry, that's just the way it is."

Solution

Management decided to replace their existing system and go with us.

Results

The bank estimates that selecting the wrong vendor initially cost them over $500,000. A painful lesson, but not nearly as painful as continuing to be strapped with an inadequate system that doesn't allow them to offer what their clients want. When I asked the executive vice president of operations at the bank about the situation he just shook his head and said, "Well, it's a whole lot cheaper if you buy right the first time."

Ask the Question

So how about you? How important is it for you to buy right the first time and avoid this painful and costly lesson?

Theme Five — Recruiting: Focus on why you work here, more income, more equity and more fulfillment

Here's a story from one of the nations leading life insurance companies:

Background

We have an agent named Dan. His dream was to teach school. Dan began teaching 8th-grade math at a local middle school after graduating from college.

Journey

Dan is one of the finest people I know. He loves kids and has a strong faith. He's the kind of person who always makes a difference. In addition to teaching, he coached football and under his leadership The Fellowship of Christian Athletes grew from ten people to more than one hundred.

Challenge

After giving one hundred percent of himself for three years Dan became disillusioned with teaching. The bureaucracy of the school was choking him and the parents of unruly children were dragging him down. No matter how hard Dan worked, his salary didn't reflect his efforts. He decided to make a change.

Solution

Dan was attracted to the financial services industry because he liked the idea of being a financial advisor and helping people make sound financial decisions. And, of course, he liked the idea of a higher income potential. Dan looked at several financial firms but he chose us because he felt like we shared his values. He told me, "I'm an entrepreneur by nature and teaching school limited me. I wanted to work with clients who were willing to take responsibility and make a change."

Results

Dan has been with us for ten years. He's a top quartile producer. He is a member of the Million Dollar Round Table (MDRT) and earns five times what he did when he was a teacher.

A few days ago I was talking with Dan and he told me that when he thinks about his career he realizes that he learned a powerful lesson. "Sometimes when you try on those dreams you had as a child, you find that they don't really fit right. When this happens you can either plug along and watch a little piece of you die each day, or you can take the risk and make a change."

He told me the best thing that he ever did was make a change while he still had the chance.

Ask the Question

So how about you? Are you willing to make a change while you still have a chance? I challenge you to think about life ten years from now, twenty years from now, even thirty years from now. Picture yourself achieving the same success as Dan and ask yourself, "Was it worth the risk to make the change?"

Theme Six — Protection: Focus on keeping me, my assets and my income safe

This story from an insurance agent highlights the value of having a good risk manager.

Background

One of my clients is a successful doctor. He and his wife live in Beverly Hills. They have two sons: one 16, one 19. I sold him his homeowner's policy and then did an insurance review. When I did the review I learned that another insurance company had both of his cars and that he didn't have a personal umbrella policy.

Journey

His goal was to keep the things that he had worked so hard for safe and sound. He wanted to make sure that he was protected, and he wanted the most efficient plan possible.

I recommended that he consolidate his coverage with us. I showed him that if we raised his deductibles slightly, I could insure both cars, his home, and include an umbrella policy for the same amount he was currently spending. He loved the plan and consolidated all his coverage with me.

Challenge

A few months later my client and his wife were away from home one evening and his 19-year-old son had friends over to their house. They were drinking. One of his friends parked his BMW in the driveway and my client's son tried to move it. He backed out of the driveway way too fast, smashed into a power pole, totaled the car, knocked the pole over and knocked the power out of the neighborhood. Total damages — $330,000.

"*...but Dad, it could have happened
to anybody...*"

Solution

Had I not done the review and noticed the gaps in his coverage my customer would have been out $330,000.

Results

My client now understands the value of having a risk manager.

Ask the Question

So how about you? Could you benefit from having a risk manager?

✣ ✣ ✣

Here's another great example that shows how a good risk advisor can keep your investments safe:

Background

One of my clients is a retired couple. Their children are grown and they have lived in the same house for thirty years. He works part time as a landscaper to supplement their retirement income.

Journey

They have been frugal and have saved a nice chunk of money. Their investment is very important to them and they don't want to expose it to market risk so they have it invested in a CD at their local bank.

Challenge

When I did their review I discovered that they have no supplemental health insurance. When I realized this I explained that their investment was at risk. Medical expenses could quickly wipe out their savings if he had an accident on a landscaping site or if either of them became ill.

Solution

They purchased supplemental health insurance from me based on the recommendation.

Results

My clients were always worried about an accident or an illness wiping out their savings. Now they're thrilled that they own health insurance and can rest assured that their investments are truly safe.

Ask the Question

So how about you? Are your assets really safe? Would you like me to do a financial review?

What if I Don't Have a Story Yet?

I was recently working with a newly-founded insurance company. Their innovative new product, SalaryShield, is designed to replace your income in the event of your death. With SalaryShield, instead of receiving a lump sum payment, you pick the amount of income you want to replace should something happen to the bread winner. It's a great concept, but it's new and prospective buyers needed an easy way to understand the product.

I was hired to help create their Client Attraction Story. Unfortunately their product is so new that they do not have a good story to tell yet. They cannot speak of problems their clients have encountered, nor can they share any solutions or results scenarios.

To create their story we created something I call the **Opposite Story**. If you don't have a hero, tell the story about a person that could have avoided hardship if they had been your client. This true story came from their head of insurance services.

Background

My brother, Ed, lived in Arlington, Texas, where he was a successful real-estate developer. Ed, his wife, Linda, and their two kids lived a very comfortable lifestyle. Not only did they own a beautiful home in Arlington, they had a vacation home on South Padre Island in the Gulf of Mexico, as well.

Journey

Ed and Linda had three goals:

1. They wanted to put their kids through college

2. They wanted to fund a comfortable retirement

3. And they wanted to set money aside for their son who is hearing impaired

Beyond that, they loved South Padre Island and once Ed retired they planned to spend as much time there as possible. They envisioned it becoming a fun gathering place for their kids and their grandkids to visit.

Obstacle

Unfortunately, my brother died when he was 52. Early on, Ed had been a smoker and he died unexpectedly, two weeks after being diagnosed with a lung disease.

Solution

Fortunately, Ed had $800,000 in life insurance. His wife, Linda, received the insurance in a lump sum payment and for a few years lived comfortably. But Linda went through the money very fast. She bought an expensive car for herself and one for each of her children. She also received some bad investment advice and due to poor market conditions lost a great deal of her money.

Results

Linda blew through her lump sum payout in just four years. To make matters worse, she has acute inflammation in her joints and is unable to work. She receives a small disability payment as well as a death benefit from Social Security but it is not nearly enough to live on. When the money was completely gone she was forced to sell their vacation home on South Padre Island and both children were forced to drop out of college to help support their mother.

Like many people, Ed and Linda would have been so much better off if they had SalaryShield. Instead of the lump sum payment, Linda would have received the equivalent of Ed's paycheck every month until the time that he would have reached age 65. If this had been the case, her lifestyle wouldn't have changed.

1. She wouldn't have bought $150,000 worth of expensive cars

2. She wouldn't have invested the remaining $600,000 in aggressive growth investments.

3. She wouldn't have lost all her money

4. Their children could have stayed in college

5. The children wouldn't have to support her now

6. She could spend her vacations on South Padre Island with her children and grandchildren

Ask the Question

So how about you? Are you concerned about your survivors blowing through a lump sum payment? Are you worried that they might get bad investment advice? Would you like to make sure that life will go on as normal, even if something happened to you?

If so, I'd be happy to you set up a SalaryShield so what happened to Ed and Linda will never happen to you.

Inserting Your Client Attraction Story into Everyday Conversation

Now that you have a great story to tell, you need to work on inserting it in everyday conversation. It's time to replace that elevator speech with a natural conversation that makes your prospect eager to learn more about your products and services. The problem with elevator speeches is that they are too long and sound too contrived. I've often heard that a good elevator speech should last thirty seconds. When you are meeting someone for the first time, thirty seconds is an eternity when describing what you do. I think there is a much better way. I call this a Client Attraction Conversation. Your goal is to deliver a WOW that engages and kindles the person's interest while opening the door for you to share more in a conversation.

The Sales Conversation

A good sales conversation has three basic parts:

1. What do you do? This is your WOW line.

2. What do you mean? This is your HOW line.

3. How do you do that? This is your Client Attraction Story.

How many times a week are you asked, "So, what do you do?" On average I bet you're asked this question at least five times a week. That's over 250 times a year. Unless you have a compelling answer, you are squandering one of your best business development opportunities.

You're probably thinking, "Yes, I do get asked that question a lot but the vast majority of those asking don't really need my products or services." Maybe they do, maybe they don't, but you cannot rule out the possibility that they know somebody who is looking for *exactly* what you provide. If they tell their friend about you, it's a referral. And when a referral comes from a friend it's the best gift you can ask for.

Unfortunately, most people answer the "What do you do?" question by simply stating their title. Responses like "I'm an accountant," "I'm an insurance agent" or "I'm in real estate" do nothing to differentiate you from the masses. When you introduce yourself like that, you are not conveying the unique value that you bring to the table. You are commoditizing yourself. You are putting yourself into a category. When you paint yourself into a category chances are the person you're talking with will think, "Oh, an accountant, I've already got one of those." They may not say that, but that's what they're thinking. Their interest is not piqued and they don't want to know any more about what you do. If you simply state the products and services you sell you are invisible. And if you do not pique curiosity and generate questions you will remain invisible.

Instead of telling people "what" you do, start with the result or outcome of what you do. For example, the accountant might say, "I help people reduce their taxes". The financial advisor might say, "I help people avoid the three biggest financial mistakes most people make". If I received an answer like that I guarantee I would follow up with, "Wow, how do you do that?" With that kind of response the person now has permission to tell his or her Client Attraction Story.

"Hey Mr. Popular, are you the guy that helps people reduce taxes?"

Your goal is to state what you do in a manner that begs the question, "Wow, what do you mean?" Think of the wow line as a two to three second elevator speech that begs the question, "How do you do that?" Your answer has to be something that uniquely describes what you do. You have to own it, you have to be completely comfortable with it, so get creative and have fun. You will most likely have to try on a few answers before you find one that truly fits. You'll know you've got it when the person you are speaking with says, "Wow, what do you mean?" or "How on earth do you do that?"

My Sales Conversation

I am a professional speaker and a sales messaging consultant, but when asked what I do for a living I respond, "I teach people the secret to attracting more clients." I've never met any business person with top line revenue responsibility that wouldn't like more clients. And so people look at me curiously and ask, "What's the secret?" I answer the question the same way every time. "There's three key parts, but the first thing you have to do is create a message that attracts clients ... I call it a Client Attraction Story." Then I'm quiet for a moment and wait to see if there is further interest. If there are no further inquiries the conversation about what I do ends there. But in most cases I'm asked, "What do you mean ... Client Attraction Story?" or "What's an example of a good Client Attraction Story?" If they ask that second question, I now have permission to tell my Client Attraction Story and I reply the same way every time, "I was recently hired by a large insurance company to go to Los Angeles and train 250 insurance agents ..."

Sample Sales Conversations

1. Here is a sample sales conversation between a prospect and a financial advisor who provides investment and retirement planning:
   - What do you do? (wow line) "I help people avoid the three biggest investment mistakes most people make."
   - What are the biggest mistakes? (how line) "The biggest mistake is lack of diversification ... it's the single biggest reason that people lose a lot of money they shouldn't lose."
   - What do you mean? (Client Attraction Story) "One of my clients is in the furniture business ..."

2. Here's a sample sales conversation between a prospect and a salesperson selling technology to small banking institutions:
   - What do you do? (wow line) "I help small banks take business from large banks."

➤ What do you mean? (how line) "I sell technology that streamlines and integrates their operation."

➤ How do you do that? (Client Attraction Story) "One of my clients is a small, but rapidly growing bank in …"

3. Here's another sample conversation between a prospect and a salesperson selling point of sale terminals to restaurants:

➤ What do you do? (wow line) "I help restaurants make more money."

➤ What do you mean? (how line) "We provide the systems that help the restaurants make better decisions."

➤ How do you do that? (Client Attraction Story) "One of my clients owns a chain of restaurants in Scottsdale …"

4. Here's another sample conversation between a prospect and a salesperson selling signage:

➤ What do you do? (wow line) "I'm a brand identity advisor."

➤ What do you mean? (how line) "We create signage designed to help our clients attract more clients."

➤ How do you do that? (Client Attraction Story) "One of our clients just built the largest facility in Philadelphia …"

5. Here's another sample conversation between a prospect and an online mortgage lender:

➤ What do you do? (wow line) "I help clients get the best mortgage at the best price."

➤ How do you do that? (how line) "We're one of Lending Tree's top lenders so we can do a couple of things most mortgage companies can't do."

➤ What do you mean? (Client Attraction Story) "One of my clients is a young couple ..."

Creating a Conversation Deficit

I f you want to make your sales conversation even more powerful there is one more step you may wish to consider.

I love to learn about people. I am fascinated by what they do, how they do it and how long they have been doing it. I love to learn what makes them successful in their field. This fascination has lead me to play a little game that I call "How Much Can I Learn About You Before You Know Anything About Me." It's always interesting to see how far I can go with it.

When I meet someone I ask typical introduction-type questions. What do you do? Where do you live? Do you have any children? What's interesting to me is that some people don't reciprocate with questions. While it's natural for me to say, "I'm from Charlotte, where are you from?" sometimes I can ask five or six questions before the person I'm speaking with asks me a question in return. I call this creating a conversation deficit. I try to keep this going for as long as possible until the person realizes that because I have been asking all the questions, they know little to nothing about me. Then suddenly they realize they are enjoying the conversation but they don't know anything about me and they naturally lead in with, "I just realized I don't know anything about you ... what do you do?" And it's an easy way to insert my Client Attraction Story.

My Chat with Jack

This happened a few months ago when I was at a cocktail party and struck up a conversation with a gentleman named Jack. I began playing my little game and learned that Jack was an investment banker with Bank of America. His job is to help commercial bankers spot investment banking opportunities among their corporate clients. It's a challenging job because commercial bankers often overlook investment opportunities. These commercial bankers have limited knowledge of what Jack's team has to offer and as a result Jack feels as if the investment banking division isn't being engaged in all the possible opportunities that exist in the commercial banking market. I went on to learn about his wife, his kids, where they live, where they go to school and where they vacation. After several minutes, Jack looked at me and said, "I've really enjoyed talking with you. By the way, what do you do?"

I said, "I teach people the secret to attracting more clients." He looked at me quizzically and asked, "What's the secret?" I replied, as I always do, "There are three key things: The most important one is to create a simple message that attracts clients. I call it a Client Attraction Story." Of course,

Jack wanted to hear more. I continued, "Jack, I'm happy to tell you, but it's kind of loud in here. Let's walk out onto the deck and I'll tell you about creating a Client Attraction Story." As Jack and I walked out to the deck I began telling my Client Attraction Story.

When I was finished, Jack said, "You know, I think we could use your help. We should have you interview some of our best commercial bankers and put together a seminar that makes it easy for the other commercial bankers to spot investment banking opportunities."

I told him that I would be delighted to help him. Then I added, "By the way, I teach people how to develop a Client Attraction Story and I just told you mine." Jack smiled and said, "Well, it definitely works!"

Part Two

Engaging Clients: Creating Questions, Ideas and Insights

Three Points of Differentiation

I t used to be enough to offer high quality service while proving that you're committed to your client's success. But in this competitive marketplace that might not be enough. One of the most powerful tools that master engagers use is differentiation. In addition to service and client commitment, the top advisors differentiate their businesses from their competition.

There are three proven ways to differentiate your business from the competition: product superiority, operational excellence and client intimacy. If you are in the business of offering advice, it's likely that the **Client Intimacy** strategy will be the most effective for you.

1. Product Superiority

Some businesses thrive by creating superior products. BMW is a classic example of a company that differentiates themselves by product superiority. Their tag line is "The Ultimate Driving Machine." People buy BMWs because they know that they are buying a superior product. They like the way the car feels; BMWs are tight, they're firm and they're engineered to perform. And while this strategy works beautifully for BMW, product superiority is a difficult way to differentiate a service firm.

2. Operational Excellence

Some businesses thrive by creating operational excellence. Wal-Mart is one of the largest companies in the world thanks in part to its operational excellence. They have dominated the big box retail market because they are masters at supply chain management. Their ability to negotiate with suppliers and manage inventory is second to none. While this works for Wal-Mart it doesn't hold up as well for people in the business of offering advice because operational excellence is expected — in fact, it's required and so is rarely a point of differentiation.

3. Client Intimacy

McKinsey & Company is a management consulting firm advising leading companies on issues of strategy, organization, technology and operations. McKinsey is a great example of a firm that has grown because of its ability to create intimate relationships with clients. McKinsey consultants invest a great deal of time and money learning about prospective clients before the initial meeting. The research they do up front provides a deep understanding of their client's situation. Armed with this knowledge about the client, McKinsey's goal is to establish a high level of intimacy so that the client feels they are in the best possible hands. When this level of intimacy is achieved price is very rarely an issue. McKinsey is frequently selected over competing firms as a result of their thorough understanding of their prospective client's strengths and weaknesses.

This third strategy, **Client Intimacy,** is the preferred strategy for anyone who makes money by offering advice.

Client Intimacy Comes From Four Areas:
1. What you know about them
2. The power questions to ask
3. The willingness to walk away
4. The ideas and insights you create together

What You Know About Them

I f you have insights into a prospective client's business or industry you will engage them on a much more meaningful level. With the right tools you are only minutes away from finding the information you need.

One of my favorite tools for learning about a prospective client's industry and the challenges they face is First Research (*www.firstresearch.com*). It's a subscription service that allows you to search hundreds of different industries to get a quick overview and learn about the challenges that industry faces.

Here's an example of how I use this tool to harness the power of **What You Know About Them**. I was recently speaking to a group of entrepreneurs who asked me to teach them how to attract more clients. Their group met once a month and they each took turns hosting the meeting. The day I spoke the meeting was being hosted by a fellow named Cliff who owned a chain of upscale fitness centers. I wanted to demonstrate the power of "what you know" to the group, so the night before the meeting I logged onto First Research and entered the search words, "Fitness Centers." A few seconds later I was looking at a twenty page report with everything you could want to know about Fitness Centers. The first paragraph was labeled **Industry Overview** and was helpful:

> "About 15,000 companies and non-profits in the U.S. operate over 26,000 fitness and recreation centers with combined annual revenue of **$15 billion**. Large companies include Bally Total Fitness, 24 Hour Fitness, and Town Sports International, operator of the Sports Clubs brand. About 5,000 centers are operated by non-profits like **YMCA**s. The industry is extremely **fragmented**: the fifty largest companies hold only about thirty percent of the market, and only a few dozen companies own more than ten centers. A typical large fitness center has $3 million of annual revenue and sixty-five employees."

But as I scrolled down the report I found what I was looking for in a section called Business Challenges. The first challenge listed was high member attrition rate:

> "**High Member Attrition Rate** — About thirty-five to forty percent of fitness club members don't renew memberships, making revenue uncertain and requiring high marketing costs to get new members."

The next day during my presentation I shared with the group that, armed with that one piece of information, I could now call Cliff and leave the following voice mail, "Hey Cliff, I've been doing some research on the fitness industry and I understand that membership attrition is one of your industries biggest challenges. I have an idea that would help you significantly reduce attrition. If you would like to hear more, let me know a convenient time to meet."

I then turned to our host and said, "Cliff, if you received that call, would you take the meeting?" Cliff quickly replied, "I would meet with you in a heartbeat!" As it turned out, Cliff had worked hard in this area and at only twenty-five percent, his club's member attrition was significantly lower than average for the fitness industry. Even though he was doing better than average in this area it was still his single biggest challenge and one that he focused on intensely. I now had Cliff's attention.

That's the power of What You Know About Them. Armed with this knowledge, I was different from most of the people who call on Cliff. Within a few seconds Cliff knew that I knew his biggest challenge. He didn't know how I knew it; he just knew that I knew it. It took me less than five minutes to log in and search for their biggest challenge and I was completely differentiated from other advisors who might call on Cliff.

Here are the five powers of What You Know About Them.

The Power of What You Know About Them:

1. Immediately gain the prospect's attention by talking about the issue they care about the most

2. Positions you as an insightful resource

3. Differentiates you from other advisors

4. Builds instant credibility

5. Allows you to focus your ideas on the prospects biggest challenge

The Power Questions to Ask

When it comes to questioning prospective clients I find that most professionals do not put enough thought into the questions they ask to get a better understanding of their customer's situation. And yet in order to be successful in the role of advisor, you must fully understand your customer's goals and be aware of the obstacles they may face. In an effort to take your practice to the next level you should develop a set of **Power Questions**. I suggest creating your five favorite Power Questions. They will evolve over time, but the key is to have a set of questions that you can rely on in the heat of the moment.

When engaging a prospective customer you should immediately assume the role of advisor by asking these Power Questions and taking a consultative approach to the conversation. Once you have a thorough understanding of the situation, your role as advisor is to help the customer overcome all of the obstacles so that they may achieve that goal.

My favorite Power Question is something I call the "Here/ There" question. To begin, I draw the following diagram:

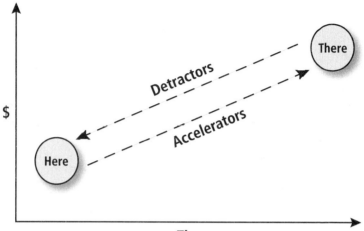

Then I say, "Let's say that you are 'Here' and over the next few years you want to get 'There.' There are certain things that will help you get 'There' faster, let's call those things Accelerators. And of course my job as your advisor is to help you get 'There' as fast as possible. There are also things that will slow you down. Let's call them 'Detractors.' My job as your advisor is to help reduce or eliminate these 'Detractors.'"

Then I ask my client four questions:

1. **Where is "There" for you?** "There" is simply the client's goal; the quest, the journey, the thing that they are trying to achieve. I let the client do most of the talking and I take notes as quickly and thoroughly as possible. When I have a good picture of "There" I summarize and synthesize what they have said. The six most powerful words you can use to start your summary are, "Here's what I heard you

say ..." When you listen intently and get it the first time, your client appreciates it and their faith in you begins to rise.

2. Once I have a good picture of "There", I go backward and ask, **"Where is 'Here' for you?"** I want to get a clear picture of their current situation. Again, I let them do most of the talking and I listen intently and summarize what I learn.

3. Once we have a good picture of "Here" and "There" I ask them, **"What are the Accelerators that will help them get 'There' faster?"** I'm still listening, but I might suggest a couple of additional Accelerators based on my knowledge of their situation and others businesses.

4. The last question I pose is, **"What are the Detractors that slow you down?"** I'm always amazed at what I learn with this question. If you have done a good job of listening and summarizing on the first three questions, your client is more than willing to bear his soul and share intimate details of foibles, distractions and missteps. Be careful not to judge; simply listen, summarize and empathize.

More Power Questions

When I interview advisors and consultants to help them develop their Client Attraction Story and their engagement process, I always ask them what questions they use when they meet with clients.

Here are three additional Power Questions that I really like:

1. One of the financial advisors I interviewed said that he asks, **"How was money treated in your family when you were growing up?"** He has learned that by asking this question his client will talk about his mother and father, what they valued, what they did right, what they did wrong and as a result what the client has come to value. He went on to say that the answers to this question give him insight on how best to work with the client and how to create an optimal investment strategy for his unique situation.

2. **"What are you truly passionate about? In other words, if you had all the money you needed, how would you spend your time?"** This is one of those questions that most people have never been asked. It causes them to really think about their priorities and their answer will enlighten the both of you.

3. Another version of this question is, **"What gives you joy?"** In the race to have more, move faster, do more and experience more, people often forget to stop and consider what really brings them joy. In most cases, it's not the big things, but rather the relationships with people or working on causes that are near and dear to them. Sometimes this answer comes in the form of their BHAG, that is, their "Big

Hairy Audacious Goal". This is a goal that is bigger than they are and requires them to stretch and invoke others to get involved.

Ask questions like these and you will be thought of as a very different kind of advisor.

Vacation Time Share

I recently had some spare time while traveling and decided to sit in on one of those short presentations on vacation time shares. I was amazed at the quality of the questions asked by the sales representative. Simple, but powerful questions such as, "Where do you and your family typically vacation?" and "If I gave you two free vacations anywhere in the world, where would you go?" and "If you could surprise your wife, where would you take her?" While I sat there envisioning crystal blue waters and tropical sunsets, the sales representative asked, "On a scale of one to ten, how important is travel to you?" She had primed me for this question as I had just admitted to her, in so many words, that travel was a *very* important part of my life. And then came the clincher, "Who plans your travel?" Like most people, I didn't have a clear definitive answer, and when I admitted that, the representative had a perfect opening to tell me about how her company eliminates this burden and serves as my travel advisor.

The Willingness to Walk Away

In order to engage clients at a high level you also must have a clear picture of who your ideal client is and what they look like. You must be clear as to what value you can and cannot bring to your client. And you must be willing to walk away if you find that your prospective client does not fit your ideal client scenario.

By asking the right questions you will be able to:

1. Establish who you can and cannot help

2. Reinforce the expertise you bring and the type of client that benefits the most

One of my clients sells technology to banks. Their ideal client is a community bank that wants to grow rapidly. In many cases, their target customers are small banks that want to grow by taking market share away from bigger banks. Using a consultative approach to engage prospects, my client often opens with three important questions:

1. On a scale of 1 to 10, how aggressive is the leadership in your bank?

2. On the same scale, how aggressively are you trying to grow the bank?

3. On the same scale, how much do you have to compete with bigger banks and take market share?

If growth and competing with bigger banks does not score high on the 1 to 10 scale, my client walks away from the deal. He knows it's a waste of time for both parties. On the other hand, if they score high numbers on the 1 to 10 scale their answer sounds something like, "I'm glad to hear that, because if you're not trying to grow and win market share then we probably aren't the right company for you."

In addition to qualifying customers, these three questions quickly position my client as the supplier that can help community banks compete with the big banks and grow their market share. It also reinforces the importance of these services.

Clearly stating such things as "If you're not trying to grow and win market share, then we probably are not the vendor for you" establishes your company's parameters and reinforces your value proposition. You may have to walk away from a few deals but you will win a higher percentage of the engagements you pursue.

Who You'll Say No to Defines Who You Are

An insurance representative once told me that sixty percent of people inquiring about insurance services do not really need what his agency offers. He told me that his job is to weed out the inquiries as quickly as possible so he can focus on the forty percent who need what he can provide.

It's important to establish up front who you are and who you are not. If the customer is not the right match you must be willing to walk away.

In Chris Zook's book *Profit from the Core* he points out a great business paradox:

> ## *"From focus comes growth; by narrowing scope one creates expansion"*

Another great example comes from the insurance agents that I mentioned in my Client Attraction Story who open the conversation by clearly stating, "If you're just looking for cheaper car insurance, I guarantee that you can find that somewhere else. But I can tell that you're successful and have accumulated some wealth over the years. If you want me to take a look at what you own and recommend the most effective way to protect it, then I'm your guy ... but you need to think of me as your risk manager and not as a provider of cheap car insurance ... is that of interest to you?"

This type of opening conversation lets the prospective client know exactly how you can help and how you cannot help.

Activity: Power Questions

Use the following two questions to help establish who you can help and who you should walk away from:

1. Who is your target market? Who is your ideal client?

   _____

   _____

   _____

2. Why do they buy from you?

   _____

   _____

   _____

Create at least two Power Questions. The questions should establish what you can do for the customer and remind him of the importance of that service.

1. _____

2. _____

The Ideas and Insights You Create Together — Six Thinking Hats

One of the most powerful ways to create client intimacy is with the ideas and insights that you create with your client. Creating ideas with your client requires you to become a good meeting facilitator. In my experience the most powerful way to facilitate a group problem solving or idea generation session is with a technique I learned in a book by Edward de Bono called *Six Thinking Hats*. I've used Dr. de Bono's process to facilitate hundreds of group brainstorming sessions which have always produced stellar results.

To facilitate an idea generation session using the *Six Thinking Hats* theory, approach the topic from the perspective of each hat, one hat at a time.

1. White Hat — the hat of knowledge. Just the facts, what we currently know.

2. Green Hat — the hat of new ideas. The more the better.

3. Blue Hat — the hat of organization. What problem do we want to solve?

4. Black Hat — the hat of caution. What could go wrong?

5. Yellow Hat — the hat of possibility. What could go right?

6. Red Hat — the hat of intuition. What is your gut feel? No need to justify with logic.

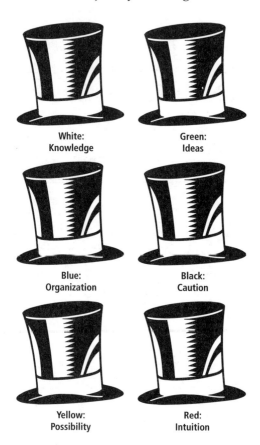

White:
Knowledge

Green:
Ideas

Blue:
Organization

Black:
Caution

Yellow:
Possibility

Red:
Intuition

Three Critical Rules for Six Thinking Hats:

1. Don't start your session until you have a clear written objective: what do we intend to accomplish in this session and what is the desired outcome?

2. During the session participants can wear only one hat at a time. If you are addressing the Green Hat (new ideas) do not allow participants to share Black Hat (risks) comments about the ideas. Black Hat comments are valuable but hold them until the group is addressing Black Hat concerns.

3. The facilitator wears the Blue Hat. This allows the facilitator to keep the meeting controlled and organized.

The process starts by writing down the goal of the brainstorming session. It is critical that you know exactly what you want to achieve. Be sure to refine the goal until everyone agrees. I like to begin with the White Hat. Write "White Hat" at the top of a flip chart and ask the group to list everything they know about the situation, being sure to stick to the facts. Within about thirty minutes the group will generate three to four flip charts filled with useful information. Each time a page from the flip chart is filled, tear it off and tape it to one of the walls of the room for the group to read and review.

When the White Hat information is completely captured write "Green Hat" at the top of a flip chart and begin brainstorming new ideas. The goal is to come up with at least twenty new ideas but don't be surprised if you come up with many more. Again, as flip charts fill up, tape the pages on the walls of the conference room.

No one has time to implement twenty new ideas, so the next step is to introduce the "Red Hat." Review all of the ideas and pick the best by allowing each participant to put a check mark beside the three ideas that they think show the most promise. Four or five of the ideas will receive the majority of the votes and will quickly emerge as the best.

Next, "Black Hat" the top vote getters to see if there are any potential pitfalls. Those ideas that are still alive must then pass the "Yellow Hat" test to determine the best possible outcome should the idea be implemented. Close the meeting with the "Blue Hat" and develop an action plan of what to do next.

It was during a recent sales call that I discovered the true power of the Six Thinking Hats: the power to make a sale. I now refer to them as the Six Hats for Sales. I received a phone call from a sales manager who wanted to create online training for his product. I suggested that we use the brainstorming technique called the Six Thinking Hats to fully explore his idea. The sales manager had never heard of the Six Thinking Hats, so I explained that it was a structured idea generation and problem solving technique. He liked the sound of it so much that he asked to bring the owner of the company to the meeting to participate in the brainstorming session.

Our goal was: How can we use online technology to recruit and retain clients? At the end of my sales call we had acquired a wealth of powerful information. The sales manager requested a copy of my notes from the session because we had created such a huge body of knowledge about his company and its clients. The notes were chock-full of the best training ideas and included everything that could go right and wrong in the process.

The next day I received a personal thank you note from the sales manager. He was thrilled with both the Six Thinking Hat process and the ideas it generated. It turned out to be an amazing sales call even though it didn't feel like a sales call at all.

Benefits of Using Six Thinking Hats in my sales call:

1. The prospect liked the idea of Six Thinking Hats and wanted to meet immediately

2. The prospect brought the owner to the meeting

3. I received valuable information that allowed me to structure the best solution

4. I never had to plug my company or its products and services

5. The client thought of me as a valuable consultant

6. The client thanked me for coming

Three Ways to Use Six Thinking Hats

When using the Six Thinking Hats exercise you quickly become an expert facilitator. You provide an organized process that people easily understand. It allows and encourages them to produce honest, thoughtful, valuable results.

Three Ways to Use the Six Thinking Hats within Your Organization:

1. Internally with teams to generate ideas or solve problems

2. Externally with clients for discovery and idea generation

3. In written and verbal follow-up conversations. You don't have to use all of the Hats and you can use one at a time. It's perfectly acceptable to say, "I'm about to meet with a client. Do you have any 'White Hat' concerns about them?"

The Six Hats can have tremendous power with your client, but it's best to practice it internally first. If you're like me, you'll be amazed with the power and efficiency of the Six Hat process and you'll naturally start using it with clients.

Before we leave the Six Hats, it's important to note why this process works so well

1. Parallel Thinking: When you ask your group to put on the "White Hat" and talk about facts, you are being very clear about the information you want. Everyone will share the facts that they know. This is known as parallel thinking. Everyone thinks in the same direction and the quantity and quality of the information you gather will be better than you ever imagined.

2. Honesty: Your group will also be more honest and candid with their comments. If I say, "Give me your 'Red Hat,'" I really want to know your personal opinion, your "gut" feel. No one has to justify their answer, they just have to tell me what they really think. If I say, "Give me your 'Black Hat,'" I'm asking for concerns. It's okay for them to tell me that they don't like something, even if it's the boss's pet project.

3. Movement Value: When the group wears only one hat at a time, you create a safe environment to create bold ideas. Don't worry that the idea is crazy or far-fetched; your crazy idea may give another person the inspiration to come up with a fantastic idea. This is known as movement value and it only happens in an environment where participants can share their ideas without fear of someone "Black Hatting" their crazy idea.

Activity: The Six Thinking Hats

Try using the Six Thinking Hats with your team. The next time you have a big challenge, facilitate a Six Thinking Hats session or appoint a team member to be the facilitator of the meeting and follow these simple steps:

1. If possible, you or your facilitator should read the book *Six Thinking Hats*. Better yet, attend a one-day training class. The class I attended was developed by Innova Training. You can contact them at *innovation@innovatraining.com*.

2. The facilitator writes the objective of the session on a flip chart or in a Word document that is being projected for all to see. Review the objective of the meeting with the group and ask if everyone agrees with the objective. If someone has a concern about the wording of the objective, discuss it with the group and reword it until everyone is satisfied.

3. Quickly review the type of thinking that you will do with each of the six hats. Remind the group that during this meeting you will only wear one hat at a time.

4. Write the words, "White Hat" and ask the group, "What do we know about this situation?" Take notes on the flip chart or in the Word document.

5. Write the words, "Green Hat" and ask, "Now that we all know what we know, what are some ideas or alternative ways to solve the problem?" Take notes on the flip chart or in the Word document.

6. When you have twenty or more ideas tell the group that you want them to put on the "Red Hat." Ask each of them to decide, in their opinion, which of the ideas will have the best impact. Give each participant three votes. Use markers if you're using flip charts or simply go around the room and ask them the number of the idea they like best and tally the votes that way.

7. Ask the group to put on the "Yellow Hat." For the ideas that got the most votes, ask the group, "What's the best thing that could happen if we implement this idea?" Do this for each of the top ideas.

8. If one of the best ideas has some "Black Hat" concerns, you may want to ask the group for some "Green Hat" ideas on how to overcome the "Black Hat" concerns.

9. Finally, the facilitator discusses the next steps with the group. What will we do next? Who will be responsible for doing it? What is our deadline?

10. Thank everyone for participating.

Observe the Real World

One of my favorite techniques for generating the ideas that clients crave is simply observing the real world. When I'm working with a new client to create a client engagement process or a compelling message, I always ask if I can interview my client's top performers. This allows me to blend best practices with proven sales strategies to create a sales approach that's easy to implement.

I've found that each top performer tends to have a unique approach. Sometimes after interviewing several people it's hard to believe that they all work for the same company. But if you talk to enough of them, a few common themes will emerge. Once I find these themes I synthesize the lessons learned into one elegant message and one simple approach.

I have found that using this interview approach results in the following:

1. It ensures that the proposal I develop is relevant and easy to implement. It's unrealistic for me to say, "Here's what I do and how I do it, now take this and

apply it to your situation." But saying, "I've talked to the top ten sales people in your organization. Let me show you their approach to this situation", makes it credible and much easier to implement.

2. The top performers thank me profusely. They are eager to share what differentiates them from everybody else in the marketplace. They have stories to share about what works for them and are often surprised that nobody has asked them about it until now.

How I Observe the Real World to Engage Clients

Several years ago I was competing with several firms for a web development project for a major retailer. The retailer had over 200 stores and wanted to completely overhaul its website to allow for online shopping. During the discovery meeting I asked, "Who is your target market?" and was told, "Affluent women between the ages of 35 to 55."

I knew the prospective client would evaluate firms based on who had the best ideas, the best insights into their business and who would come back with the best recommendations. To develop the best presentation and proposal I took a random sample of twenty affluent women between the ages of 35 to 55 and asked what they would like from the retailer's website. I asked what it would take to make the site worthy of them visiting it on a regular basis. I asked what would make them bookmark the site. And I asked what might be the most helpful thing the retailer could do to make the women feel welcome and valued.

After conducting my interviews I had a list of over twenty things that affluent women wanted from that retailer's website. When we delivered our proposal to the retailer I started my presentation with, "I researched your target market by interviewing twenty affluent women between the ages of 35 to 55 and made a list of everything they wanted from your website." Then I asked the group, "Would you like to know the number one thing that your target market wants?" You could have heard a pin drop. Everyone leaned forward and the lead buyer inquired, "Yes, I would love to know!" Turns out, the number one thing that those women wanted was notification of sales. They told me that they shopped at the store on a regular basis and spent a lot of money and felt as if they should be part of an elite group — notified by e-mail — about upcoming sales events. The retailer was impressed that I took the time to understand the needs and wants of their target market and they were impressed with my findings.

A few days later I received a call saying that we had been selected to develop the site. The retailer felt that we were the only group that had a thorough understanding of their target market and were confident that we would deliver a website of value. We had observed the real world and applied what we had learned. In doing so we successfully differentiated ourselves from the other web developers. The retailer was confident that we would deliver the best of what was happening in their industry in the form of a user-friendly website.

Activity: Observing the Real World

1. List the biggest prospective engagements you are working on right now.

   _____

   _____

Note: Be sure to only include your biggest prospects. The process of interviewing and observing takes time and effort. You want to spend the time on large organizations to ensure that at the end of the day you have a valuable product that can be sold to this and other organizations.

2. Identify the people you should interview/observe to better understand and create a solution for the client.

   _____

   _____

Part Three

Becoming the Trusted Advisor: Creating Passion for What You Do

Authentic Enthusiasm and the Life Boat

The third tool to master in your quest to attract and engage clients is something I call **Authentic Enthusiasm.** It is an essential element in business development — quite possibly the single most important element. Authentic Enthusiasm is the conviction to believe in yourself and the desire to share the expertise that you've gained with others.

When you're filled with the power of Authentic Enthusiasm, you interact with clients on a whole new level. Because you have both proficiency and confidence, you no longer fixate on making a sale; instead, you concentrate on working with a prospective customer to implement a plan that you know will achieve the desired results. Authentic Enthusiasm radiates through every phone call, every presentation, every gesture, every voice message and every e-mail. Authentic Enthusiasm speaks louder than words.

Unfortunately, Authentic Enthusiasm is probably the most elusive element to attain in sales. It cannot be manufactured or feigned, it must be genuinely achieved. And while it doesn't happen overnight, I have found two ways to help bring about Authentic Enthusiasm. Once achieved, you will convey this powerful feeling to others through your actions and it will be hard to contain your enthusiasm.

The first way to arm yourself with the power of Authentic Enthusiasm is by telling your Client Attraction Story. When told well, your Client Attraction Story underscores the value you bring to the market. If you recall, my Client Attraction Story wraps up like this:

> At the end of my seminar two gentlemen walked up and said, "I can't believe how easy it was to follow your seminar!" And the next day I received a phone call from my client saying, "Bill, you won't believe this, I'm getting calls from agents who are no longer just quoting, but rather asking more questions and positioning themselves as risk managers. They tell me that they are not only closing more autos, but they also closing more lines per customer."

Customer Advocacy

E ach time I tell that story I'm reminded of the value I brought to my client that day. It impels me to believe in myself and all that I have to offer. My Client Attraction Story provides me with the feeling of Authentic Enthusiasm and helps me be the very best salesperson that I can be. Once you possess Authentic Enthusiasm you are no longer selling — you are simply helping clients.

Authentic Enthusiasm is unmistakable. When you have it, it permeates everything you say and do. It gives you the wherewithal to propose meetings, visit places and encounter people you might not ever have had the opportunity to meet had you not been filled with Authentic Enthusiasm. Attaining a level of Authentic Enthusiasm brings great power to your sales message. You will find that others are compelled to take action because of your energy.

The best way I can describe the feeling of Authentic Enthusiasm is to use the example of a lifeboat. Picture my prospective clients treading water while I'm in a lifeboat throwing them life jackets as fast as I can. Some of the prospects will accept my offer to help and grab onto the life jacket for dear life. Others will choose to ignore my offer to help. When they choose to continue to tread water instead of swimming toward a life jacket, I'm not offended. However, I am disappointed that I won't be given the chance to help because I'm confident that I could have provided a beneficial service.

*"Life jackets, I got life jackets,
who wants a life jacket?"*

When you fully believe in your products and services and you have the ability to help your clients, you are in the lifeboat. And being in a position to help is the most powerful position to be in when making a sale. When you've attained lifeboat status you become a customer advocate who wants the best for your customer.

But remember, you cannot fabricate your enthusiasm. If you do, you will find that it only lasts so long and takes you so far before prospective clients begin to see through it. It must be heartfelt and I believe your Customer Attraction Story will help you get there.

The Other Side of Selling

A nother equally powerful way to develop Authentic Enthusiasm is through innovation. In Part Two of this book, I presented several proven ways to consistently develop better, bolder, more actionable ideas; ideas that your clients appreciate and value, and at the same time, fill *you* with Authentic Enthusiasm.

I first felt the power of Authentic Enthusiasm years ago when my second company, Mindblazer, partnered with Yahoo to work with Purina Pet Foods. We were experts in education-based marketing, a process which focuses on talking about what your audience wants to learn, rather than what you want to sell. We worked with Purina and came up with a brilliant concept called "Six Signs of Optimal Pet Health" and produced a four-minute video package which received rave reviews. To create the program, we recruited a veterinarian and put up a banner in a park offering a FREE pet health analysis. We shot video as the vet showed pet owners six key factors for examining their pet's health. The content was powerful. Anyone who watched it immediately knew what to look for and how to keep their pet in top condition. The project was a huge success.

The whole experience was like a lunar eclipse for me. I was overflowing with Authentic Enthusiasm and immediately called four people to share my experience. From those four calls I generated four sales. I attribute my success in closing those deals to the fact that when I shared my experience I was oozing with Authentic Enthusiasm. I could hardly contain my excitement and pride.

And yet, when I shared my experience with those four prospective clients, it didn't feel like I was making a sales call. I had crossed over to the other side of sales and was simply sharing how I had *helped* my customer. It was a powerful position to be in and the first time I realized that Authentic Enthusiasm was a tool that would enable me to attract and attain clients.

Sharpening Your Creative Capacity

M ost people think that you have to be born with creative ability. The truth of the matter is that you can sharpen your creative capacity if you know the steps to follow. Allow me to share my story of creating and developing a sales and marketing idea that turned out to be a diamond. It is a good example of how we implemented a simple solution to an otherwise hopeless situation.

The Cutest Screen I've Ever Seen

It was 1990 and my small company was in the process of developing a training program for the new Mac operating system. We had never developed a software product before and this was our big chance. Savannah River Nuclear Plant hired us to create the training program for their 11,000 Macintosh users. In return for a lower development price, we negotiated ownership of the program. It was our first product of its kind. Our client expected a fun, non-intimidating interactive multimedia training program and we were poised to deliver.

Aristotle   Sir Isaac Newton   Leonardo Da Vin

We decided on cell animation and created a program that we named, "System 7: The Movie." It starred Leonardo da Vinci, Sir Isaac Newton and Aristotle. Each of these great thinkers explored the operating system from their point of view. Da Vinci looked at the new creative capabilities, Newton explored its connectivity and Aristotle examined the organization of the program. Our plan was to distribute it on CD-ROM and sell the product for $150

The energy in the room was electric as our team of five worked long hours to meet our deadline. We were determined to have our product ready in time to piggyback Apple's launch of the System 7. We were cruising right along when out of nowhere, we hit a brick wall. We reached that painful place where the excitement wears off, but there is still a long road before completion. Our project manager, spurred by exhaustion, demanded, "What we are doing here? We're working around the clock to develop a product that we're not even sure we can sell!" I tried to appear calm, but my heart sank. I knew he was right. I had no idea how we were going to sell a CD-ROM.

We were a custom shop and I was not only the owner, but the main salesman. We were trying to birth a product that was totally different from anything we had done before and we needed an entirely new approach. I knew I had to rally the troops, but what can you say or do when your lead project manager is exhausted and thinks the project is futile? I stood there, frozen for a moment, leaving a long pregnant pause while I thought of a way to restore credibility and save the day. And then it came to me, "I don't have a plan for exactly how we're going to sell this thing, but I have a plan for how we are going to come up with some ideas. I need everybody in the conference room. Now."

At the top of the dry erase board I wrote, "Twenty Ways to Sell System 7: The Movie". And gave the team their marching orders, "For the next sixty minutes we are going to brainstorm twenty different ways to sell our System 7: The Movie." The ideas came slowly at first, but before long they started coming faster and faster. When the hour was up, we had more than twenty ideas. Most of them would never work, but one idea was brilliant. It was the diamond of the bunch. Someone suggested getting *Mac Week Magazine* to review our program. It would cost us nothing, we could do it immediately and we might be able to attain their five star software rating in the process. Yes, this idea was definitely a diamond!

I walked out of the conference room, picked up the most recent copy of *Mac Week Magazine* and flipped through it until I found the name of the Technology Editor, Henry Knorr. I went to my desk and nervously dialed his number. To my astonishment Henry answered, "Yeah, what do you want?" My knees were shaking, but I managed to get the words out, "Hi Mr. Knorr, my name is Bill Whitley and I've developed a fun, non-intimidating training program for the new Mac operating system." He was half listening when he asked, "Yeah, something you plan on selling?" I replied, "Yes sir, we're going to put it on CD-ROM and sell it for $150. It stars Leonardo da Vinci, Sir Isaac Newton and Aristotle." When Henry heard that, he managed a chuckle. He asked me a few more questions and then asked me to send him a sample of the product.

We quickly sent him a few screen shots for his review and the next day Henry called and left this message, "Bill, this is Henry Knorr, I got your CD. Congratulations, that's the cutest screen I've ever seen. We're going to put your program on the cover." With this bit of luck — not to mention long hours, a lot of hard work and creativity — we went on to sell several thousand copies of "System 7: The Movie".

I like to share this story because it illustrates the power of creativity and innovation. It took us one hour to come up with the idea to get our software reviewed and that one idea netted us a huge sale. That's the power of creativity and innovation; they can be consistently developed and summoned when you need them most. It's not rocket science; in fact, it's usually one simple idea that is easy to implement and shines like a diamond.

Acre of Diamonds

After hearing that story, people will usually ask, "But, how did you know to do that? How did you know the best answer to your project manager's question was to brainstorm twenty ideas?" The answer to that question is that I'm a collector. I like to collect stories and one of my favorite stories is called "Acre of Diamonds" by Dr. Russell Conwell. Dr. Conwell lived 140 years ago. He was a Baptist Minister who went on to found Temple University. In order to raise the money to found Temple University, Dr. Conwell told the Acre of Diamonds story over 6,000 times. I first heard his story on a tape almost twenty years ago. I'm sure my version differs from the original, but here is the story as I remember it. I credit this story for getting our product on the cover of *Mac Week Magazine*.

There once was a South African, third generation farmer who worked hard and made a good living but was never completely satisfied. The farmer watched as a steady stream of foreigners came to South Africa to strike it rich in the diamond mining business. While the farmer lived a comfortable lifestyle, it was the result of back breaking work and he resented those who got rich quick with little effort.

Before long he had grown weary of working like a dog with little to show for it, so he sold his farm and took a stab at the diamond mining business. He studied the business, bought a diamond mine and began his quest. Unfortunately, Lady Luck was not on his side and he never found a single diamond. In a few years he was completely broke. The guilt of having squandered his family's fortune overwhelmed him and he eventually took his own life.

Months later the new owner of the farm came across a nice looking stone while fishing in a creek on the grounds. When he got home he put it on the mantle piece. That night his neighbor joined him for dinner and when the neighbor saw the stone he asked where he had found it. The farmer replied, "Down in the creek, why?" His neighbor said, "That's the largest uncut diamond I've ever seen." To which the farmer replied, "No kidding, there's a whole creek full of them down there."

Dr. Conwell went on to add, "The moral of the story is that before you mine everyone else's acre of diamonds, mine your own acre."

You see, as humans we all have a rich resource, our own acre of diamonds; it's called our brain. We have the ability to think, create and solve. Unfortunately, as humans we are also creatures of habit and the last thing we want to do is push ourselves to think outside the box. When faced with a problem, it seems easier to seek the opinions of others than delving into a solution on our own.

Dr. Conwell said, "The next time you are faced with a challenge, instead of asking others what they would do, sit down in a quiet place with a piece of paper and a pen and make a list. At the top of the sheet of paper write the words, "Twenty ways to grow my business" or "Twenty ways to live a healthier lifestyle" or "Twenty ways to be a better father." Don't be afraid if eighteen or nineteen of your ideas are useless, because one or two will probably be diamonds."

I'd like to tell you that I use this technique every day, but I don't. But, when I'm faced with a big challenge, I find myself drawn to a quiet place with a legal pad and pen trying to come up with twenty solutions. This technique works for me; I manage to come up with better solutions to my challenges and over time I believe I have built my mental muscle. I've noticed that the more I do this exercise, the better I get at it. I come up with more ideas, bigger ideas and I'm much faster at reaching my goal of twenty solutions. If you exercise your biceps your arms will become toned and stronger and you will most definitely be happy with the results. The same goes for your brain; if you exercise your brain you will also see results and I think you'll like them just as much.

Activity: Finding your Diamonds: 20 Ways to …

What are Your Diamonds?

Identify a problem or challenge.

_____

_____

List at least twenty ways to address your challenge. Don't stop and analyze or think through any of the ideas until you have finished. Keep your mind open and list as many ideas as you can. When you're done, go back over the list and pick the diamonds. The ideas that are easy to implement and will have immediate impact.

Creating an Idea Bank

By now, I hope you're getting the message that creativity and innovation can be developed and harnessed. If you follow the steps you've just learned, you'll create better and more valuable ideas. You'll create diamonds and your clients will appreciate you more. To make sure you have a place to keep all the ideas, I have developed a concept I call an **Idea Bank**.

"The palest ink is stronger than the best memory"

I'm sure you have seen an Indian Dream Catcher, those feathery things that catch dreams at night. I like to think of my laptop as an idea catcher. Ideas will come and go, and once they're gone, they're gone forever. An Idea Bank allows you to capture, collect and organize your ideas. Once in your bank, the ideas are stored forever and you can call upon them as needed.

The main point of the Idea Bank is to have a single place where all the things that you learn can be filed. Organize it any way you like, but store it electronically. This allows you to have everything at your fingertips with the ability to retrieve it easily whenever it is needed.

As you can see from this diagram, there are eight types of information that go into my Idea Bank.

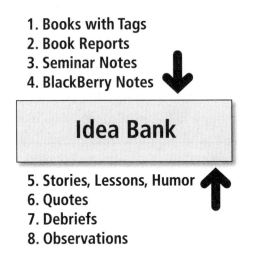

1. **Books with Tags**
2. **Book Reports**
3. **Seminar Notes**
4. **BlackBerry Notes**

Idea Bank

5. **Stories, Lessons, Humor**
6. **Quotes**
7. **Debriefs**
8. **Observations**

Books with Tags

The first things that go into my Idea Bank are books with tags. One of the best business books I've ever read is *Love is the Killer App* by Tim Sanders. If you read this book, you will never read another business book the same way. Sanders suggests that you "tag" your book. In other words, when you come across an "aha moment" in addition to underlining the section, actually turn to the front of the book and find one of those blank pages that every book seems to have and actually write down the page number and reference the "aha moment". Describe the main thought or idea that was generated from the passage. It doesn't have to be anything fancy, simply capture "the aha" moment in its truest form.

You will notice a couple of interesting things when you "tag" a book. First, the book will look and feel more like an idea catalogue. It now contains a wonderful list of ideas and it references the exact page to read, review and remember. Second, you now have a deeper connection with the book. You didn't just read the book, you interacted with it. You looked for good ideas and you wrote each one down. It's the difference in hearing a good joke and remembering a good joke. And last, once you've tagged a book, you'll never give it away. You've enhanced it. It is now your idea catalogue and you'll want to keep it handy. I challenge you to try it. If you do, you'll turn every good business book you read into an "Idea Catalogue."

Sanders also makes the point that you can't read all the books that are published, so spend some time to ensure that the ones you read are the best. Listen for book recommendations from friends, check out the official lists of bestsellers, and search key words that are of interest to you. If a book shows up in two or more of those places, you know you've got a winner.

Once you read a book, share your knowledge. When you have a conversation with a client or business associate experiencing a challenge and you're reminded of a book, recommend the book! Share the good books you read with your clients and prospects. Sharing your knowledge and the books that you got the knowledge from builds relationships.

Book Reports:

When I finish reading a book and it's still fresh in my mind, I write a brief one to two page outline and highlight the key lessons learned. I summarize the key messages from the book and enter the book report into this folder for quick retrieval.

Seminars Folder:

I enjoy listening to the best professional speakers I can find. Sometimes I attend live seminars, other times I listen to seminars on CD. I always take notes to keep the ideas and key messages alive.

In the past I took notes and kept them in a spiral notebook but I've found that when I type the notes directly into my laptop they're more complete, more organized and easier to track down when I want them.

BlackBerry Notes:

If I'm in a meeting or someplace where it's inappropriate to have a laptop, I use my BlackBerry to take notes. The BlackBerry is the ultimate portable miniature note-taking device. The BlackBerry syncs with Microsoft Outlook, so every note that I have on my BlackBerry also shows up on my laptop and becomes a part of my idea bank. Best of all I can just type a few letters of the name of the note and the right note pops up.

Idea Capture

Stories, Lessons and Humor:

I love to collect stories whether they're my own or stories I've heard others tell. Some of them are fully developed and completely written, others contain just the gist of the story that will later be developed into a full-fledged story. I categorize and label the stories based on the message or the lesson learned.

Particularly important are funny things that happened. I don't want to forget them or let them get away. They are priceless. For example, one time my family was hiking up a mountain path that led to a beautiful waterfall. We passed an elderly couple coming down the trail and my wife asked, "Is the waterfall pretty?" The old fellow replied, "Purty ain't the word." We still laugh about it and often repeat the phrase "Purty ain't the word."

Quotes:

This folder contains only one document. It's a long running list of great quotes and their authors. When I see or hear a quotable quote, I write it down immediately. It helps to keep the wisdom I hear in other's voices alive.

Debriefs:

The most valuable lessons you learn often come in the form of honest feedback. At the end of any meeting, if possible, I like to debrief with my client. I ask two simple questions, "What went well?" and "What could be improved?"

If you're on a joint sales call, the minute you get away, ask your colleague the same questions: what went well and what needs improvement. This gives the person permission to give thoughtful, honest, constructive criticism.

Observations:

Observations are one of the most powerful idea generators. I mentioned earlier in my Client Attraction Story that I was hired to deliver a sales seminar to a large insurance company. They told me that an average agent could write fifteen auto policies a month and their top agents could write 60 to 80 auto policies a month. To prepare for the seminar, I quickly asked if I could interview their top ten agents. I call this "observing the real world." I spent well over an hour on the phone with each agent taking notes a fast as I could. The insights I gained were fantastic. I went on to create a seminar called, "Eight Secrets of the Top Performing Agents" that was a huge success. All of the notes I took are now in my idea bank stored in a folder called observations. I could never have developed that seminar if I hadn't known how to observe the real world.

*"Yes! I found it...Now
I have to remember what I need it for..."*

Activity: Creating a Personal Idea Bank

Create an Idea Bank of your own.

1. Begin using the tagging method to catalog the key points of whatever book you are currently reading.

2. Set up an Idea Bank folder on your laptop.

3. Start creating Idea Bank files to save in this folder. Create a file every time you attend a meeting, seminar or talk with someone on the phone. Get in the habit of taking notes electronically and collecting and saving ideas.

Add stories, humor, quotes and observations to your Idea Bank. Set aside time to work on your Idea Bank every day.

Part Four

Expanding Your Presence and Extending Your Sphere of Influence

Thought Leadership

Once you have developed several good Client Attraction Stories you can easily weave them together into a powerful seminar and an article or two. Your seminars and articles are a great way to position yourself as the dominant thought leader in your market. Being the thought leader will evolve into the role of expert or trusted advisor in your industry. The more you get your name out there in the marketplace, the more people will look to you as a leader and someone they want on their team.

*"...and in conclusion: all you
need is Love!"*

Step One — Your Article

Start by writing one article. One subject to write about might be, "Three Financial Mistakes Most People Make," if you are in the financial services industry. It doesn't have to be long; most publications are looking for articles between 500 to 1,000 words. If you're not a good writer, or don't have the time to write an article, just make an outline and hire a local writer to help you polish up the article.

Once the article is written make a list of every publication in your market that might run your article, such as the local business journal, local trade association newsletters, civic organization newsletters, neighborhood association newsletters, etc. With a little effort you should be able to come up with at least twenty publications. If you fall short, type the name of your city, state, and the word "newsletter" in Google and you will have hundreds of local newsletters at your fingertips.

Once you have your list of the most desirable publications, e-mail your article to the publication editor. It helps to put a short description of yourself in the cover letter and why you think this is an important topic. Invite the editor to call you with any questions and follow up if you don't get a response.

Step Two — Your Seminar

Once your article is published it's time to make another list. This time your list should include local organizations that host speakers at their meetings. Your list should include every Rotary Chapter and Kiwanis Club as well as local chapters of trade organizations such as, American Marketing Association and Business Marketing Association. Consider including local investment clubs and church groups as well. If you need more organizations ask your clients, friends, neighbors and business associates which meetings they attend and whether or not they bring in local speakers. Once you have your list, prioritize it based on size and suitability of the audience, then call around to find the name of the person responsible for booking speakers.

Seven Tips for Developing your Seminar

1. When developing your seminar be sure to include two or three Client Attraction Stories. As you have learned, stories make the content easier to understand and easier to remember.

2. Keep your seminar short. Rotary and Kiwanis want speakers to talk for about 20 minutes. Industry specific groups are longer — maybe 45 minutes with time for questions and answers at the end.

3. Create a catchy title that conveys value. I like a title with lists such as; "Three Biggest Mistakes..." or "Three Secrets to..." or "Five Ways to... "

4. Let the audience laugh a few times. You don't have to tell a joke. Just pick a personal story that has a funny element. Tell the story and then share the lesson you learned. This is often the most retold element from your seminar.

5. Don't try to teach too many lessons with your stories. The rule is one story, one lesson. Remember Aesop's Fables: he never said "The three morals of this story are ..."

6. Meaningful visuals are wonderful. Maybe it's a chart or graph that simplifies the situation you're addressing.

7. Practice your speech and then make refinements. If you have a video camera put it on a tripod, press record and deliver your speech. This is a humbling step, but it will motivate you to refine and polish your presentation.

Step Three — Your One Page Flier

The last step is creating a one page information sheet with the title of your seminar. I recommend using the same title as your article. Include the main points that you cover in your seminar as well as your picture and bio. Mail or e-mail your one pager flier along with a copy of your published article to the appropriate person in each organization. Of course, always remember to follow up your e-mails with phone calls.

I have used this three step process to grow both of my businesses and as a result have spoken to dozens of local organizations as well as some national organizations. I've come to expect that at the end of the seminar at least three people will approach me and say, "I think we could use your services. Would you come deliver that same presentation to our management team?" And of course my answer is always, "Yes, I'd be delighted to help."

Activity: Becoming a Thought Leader

1. Considering your expertise, list two or three topics that would make good seminars for you to lead.

2. Pick one of these topics and write a summary outline for the seminar.

3. Turn your outline into an article or hire a local writer to help.

Making Your Story Available 24/7

O ne more way to leverage the power of your Client Attraction Story is to consider producing it as a video. Thanks to the Internet you can create what I call a video story package and deliver it to anyone, anywhere, anytime.

When it comes to creating a video, many corporate communicators aim a camera at an expert on the subject matter and shoot the "talking head" video. Unfortunately, it usually fails to capture an audience. Television is partially to blame for its inefficiency as our audiences have become spoiled thanks to TV's expert story telling prowess. Informational television content is built around story packages, meaning a reporter interviews several people, adds voiceover and edits the footage into a package.

A typical video story package contains a variety of characters with different points of view making it more interesting and credible than if it were presented by one corporate spokesperson. Video story packages typically run two to three minutes. They are designed to be light and easy to understand.

The characters in the video include heroes, luminaries, experts and sometimes a host.

Hero

In a good story, your client (the hero) shares their story. They will cover the same parts of the story that are in your Client Attraction Story. They start off by describing a little of their background, then they talk about their goal, what got in the way, how they overcame the obstacle (with your help) and the results. The hero captures the knowledge you're trying to share and brings it to life for the audience. Clients speak in terms that prospective clients understand while increasing the inherent drama of the video. Viewers get pulled in and become curious to find out how the hero dealt with the same challenges they face.

Luminary

The video story package should also include comments from a luminary. Luminaries are third-party experts who do not work at your company. Maybe they have written a book on the subject or done extensive research. Theoretically they are unbiased and are perfect for giving the big picture. At the appropriate point in the hero's story you can cut in with the luminary who might say something like, "Actually, the Smith's are typical of what's going on in America. Millions of people are beginning to implement ..."

The beauty of the luminary is they can give the big picture and with it they can deliver the "ship's leaving the dock, don't be left behind" message. The luminary creates a sense of urgency and safety.

Expert

The video story package should include comments from the company's expert. This is you. The role of the expert is to clearly explain how you help clients like the ones you just heard from. I refer to this as "the problem we solve" message. The expert doesn't need to sell. All the selling has been done by the hero and luminary. The expert merely needs to be likeable and credible and deliver "the problem we solve message."

Host

There is one optional person to consider in your video: the host. The host is a professional spokesperson that can serve as the glue that holds the story together. The host provides the teasers, the story set up and any concluding or summary remarks. Hosts are particularly helpful if your hero tended to ramble and you need to edit out long takes and have the host summarize the key points.

Energy

Be sure to cast people with high energy in your videos. You want to feature people who are passionate about their topic and are willing to talk about it with zeal. Unfortunately, some experts estimate that video can diminish people by up to thirty percent. In other words, if someone delivers a high-energy presentation in person, it may come across as normal energy on video. So be sure to turn up the energy to ensure effectiveness.

Using Your Video Story Package

Once you have shot and edited your video story package, have your web developer encode it and make it available on your website. But don't stop there. The real power of a video story package comes from using it to reach out to prospective clients.

Here are a few ideas to consider:

1. Send an e-mail to all of your prospective clients that reads something like this: We just helped a client achieve incredible results. If you would like to know more, just click the link below and view a short three minute video that explains how we helped. If you're interested, give me a call and we can discuss this further.

2. Put your video on DVD and package it up with a professional label and graphics. Send the DVD to all of your prospective clients with a message similar to the e-mail in idea #1 above.

3. Print a business card sized ad with a picture of the hero from the video on one side. Be sure to include the title of the video above the hero's picture with the caption, "Watch video." On the back of the card, in a few bullet points, let the viewer know

what they will learn and provide the website they should visit to see the video. Hand these out with your business card and encourage your prospective client to watch the video.

4. Give your DVD and/or video business card out at trade shows, meetings and conferences. Research shows that most people will not throw a DVD away as its perceived value is $10 to 20.

5. Put a link to your video on your e-mail signature line with the language, "We just helped our client make a million bucks ... click this link to learn how."

These are just a few ideas. I'm sure you'll come up with even more ideas. If you create a video story package that you like, e-mail me at *bill@billwhitley.com* and let me take a look. I'm always looking for good examples to share with my clients. I'd also like to hear how you're using the video and how it's working for you.

Optimizing Introductions

S uccessful advisors get the lion's share of their new business from happy clients who introduce them to their friends, family and neighbors. An introduction to a friend is the highest compliment that you can receive. It means you are succeeding on many levels.

Fredrick Reicheld makes this point brilliantly in his book, *The Ultimate Question*. He points out that if you want to truly know how well you're doing with your clients, ask this simple question: "On a scale of one to ten, how likely are you to recommend us to a friend?" A client who answers nine or ten is considered a promoter. If the answer is seven to eight, consider that client passive. And the client who answers between zero and six is a detractor.

After asking this question, add up how many promoters and detractors you have. Subtract the detractors from the promoters and you are left with your Net Promoter Score, or NPS. Your goal of course is to continually seek to increase your Net Promoter Score. The higher the score, the happier your clients are. And the happier your clients are, the more likely they are to introduce you to their friends. Think of an introduction as a reward for good service. And as Reicheld points out, they're not only a reward, they're a good barometer for how well your business treats its clients.

Although most advisors appreciate and understand the value of introduction, few of the advisors I talk to have a systematic approach for optimizing their potential. And since introductions are the number one source of new business, optimizing their potential results is a huge payoff.

The Economics of Introductions

What are the odds that if you pick up the phone and make one hundred cold calls that you will make ten sales? The odds, I'm afraid, are not very good. Perhaps you might actually speak with ten people (but most likely far less), and maybe — just maybe — you might wind up doing business with one of those one hundred people, but the thought of making all those calls overwhelms me.

Optimization is all about leverage and your greatest leverage happens when your clients are working for you. Here are three proven ways to harness the power of introductions.

Step One — Assume Success

The first step in creating an introduction-rich environment is assuming success. This means making your clients aware of how much you appreciate introductions up front. Right from the start assume that your association with the client will result in a successful relationship. Have the confidence to believe that the end result will be a positive experience for both of you. This confidence is a result of your Authentic Enthusiasm.

It's an easy habit to create. Early in the relationship educate clients that you appreciate introductions with a comment like, "I'm delighted we're going to be working together and I know you're going to be thrilled with the results that we will deliver. I want to let you know that the only way we grow our business is when happy clients tell their friends about us. So if you like what we do, please tell your friends about us."

Notice this is different than asking "who do you know that could benefit from my service?" Early in the relationship I suggest a mere statement, "we appreciate introductions" vs. "who do you know?"

After hearing this advice, one of my clients added the following to his e-mail signature line: "The greatest compliment I can receive is the introduction of your friends, family and business associates. Thank you for allowing me to serve you." This is a powerful way to automatically make clients aware of how much you appreciate introductions.

Step Two — Moments of Joy

Another good time to remind clients how much you appreciate introductions is during those "moments of joy." These are the moments when your client is extremely pleased with something that you have delivered. Harness these "moments of joy" and make introductions a natural, easy part of your marketing plan.

Suppose your client is delighted about something you have done and offers to buy you a steak dinner as his way of showing his gratitude. A steak dinner is a nice gesture, but keep in mind that if you receive an introduction that leads to new business, you will be able to buy yourself a steak dinner and then some! Perhaps you might respond by saying, "Thank you so much for your kind offer, but there is actually something that you could do that would mean even more to me. The only way we succeed is when happy clients tell their friends about us, so if you could introduce me to a couple of people who might benefit from what we do, I would be much obliged."

Step Three — Create Easy Ways for Clients to Introduce You

Steps One and Two are easy ways to get the process started, but Step Three is where you can really move the needle. As Norm Trainor, CEO of The Covenant Group, taught me, the most successful advisors create a series of events that make introductions happen at a much greater rate. One of his clients has partnered with a local golf pro to offer a series of afternoon golf clinics. He invites six of his clients to attend one of the free golf clinics. The only request is that each client brings a friend who enjoys golf and would enjoy meeting him. It's a fun experience that everyone enjoys, and a great excuse to get together. He met over thirty new clients last year with this series of events. Another one of Norm's clients is a huge Penn State football fan. Before every home game he has an elegant tailgate party with great food, drinks and fun activities. He picks clients that enjoy college football, gives them each two tickets and asks them to come to his tailgate party with a friend that would enjoy meeting him.

Keep It Friendly

You will notice that all three of these techniques are easy to accomplish, low pressure tactics. In all three cases you're not asking for a specific name — you're simply letting the client know that you appreciate introductions as a way to grow your business and you're providing an easy way to make introductions happen.

I remember talking with a financial advisor who told me about a time he was having lunch with a long-time client and he mentioned how much he appreciated introductions. His client replied, "I had no idea you wanted me to introduce you to my friends. I assumed you had all the clients you wanted." The advisor then confided to me that even though he knows introductions are important, he seems to forget to ask. He added that when he does remember to ask it usually results in several excellent introductions, further proving the point that the introduction process should be incorporated into your overall business plan.

Deeper Client Relationships

Norm Trainor also shares that there is one other huge benefit of asking for introductions. "After someone purchases, it's natural for them to second guess themselves and wonder if they made the right decision. By working with the friends and associates of your clients, you're reinforcing the idea that your client has done the right thing — if their friends are doing it, it must be right. Also, you're increasing your clients' investment in your relationship. They're now tied to you, not simply as a client, but also as a friend of another client. You have now built a network where each party is connected directly and indirectly. Your new client is grateful to your old client. Your old client is grateful to you for helping a friend. And you're grateful to your old client for helping you gain a new client."

Can you feel the love?

Activity: Introductions

1. Develop a proactive introduction statement you can use at the beginning of a client relationship.

   _____

   _____

   _____

2. Develop an introduction statement you can use during "moments of joy."

   _____

   _____

   _____

3. Make a list of things you enjoy doing — golf, football games, etc., that would lend themselves to a series of client introduction events.

_____

_____

_____

Part Five

Final Thoughts

Coaching Employees

One of the questions I hear over and over again is, "OK, I get it, I'm excited, but how do I get my team on board? How do I help them so that they can help me?"

In my experience I've found that the most powerful tool for coaching employees is using the "Here/There" power question. Simply draw out the diagram on page 92 and start the coaching process by getting a thorough understanding of where your team is and where they ought to be. Let your team do most of the talking, but feel free to chime in when you need to clarify.

Next, make it clear that your job as their manager is to help them get from "Here" to "There" as quickly and efficiently as possible. Acknowledge that you want to help them maximize the "accelerators" and minimize the "detractors." Have them describe in detail what accelerators they need to achieve their goals. Ask them to put words to the term "detractors." What is it specifically that's holding them back?

At the end of the coaching session you should have developed a list of agreeable steps that will get your team where they need to be. Finally, be sure to keep your word by following through on your commitments as well as making time to review their progress.

Strategic Visioning

Another powerful way to share your vision and gain team buy-in is with a tool I call **Strategic Visioning**. You often hear about the importance of mission statements, but rarely do you meet an employee who can recite his company's mission statement from memory. And it's even less likely to find an employee who actually uses his company's mission statement to help guide him in the decision making processes.

I think there is a much better way and I call it Strategic Visioning. Instead of describing your mission with words, try using a diagram. Create a simple visual that you and your employees can refer to when making decisions. One of the best examples of this type of diagram comes from the book *Good to Great* by Jim Collins.

According to Collins, the Hedge Hog Tool has guided many companies, taking them from being *good* at what they do to being *great* at what they do. He refers to the tool as a Hedge Hog because when threatened, a hedge hog has

"No...I can not see the future..."

one simple, but effective defense that always works: it simply raises its prickly spines to fend off predators. Likewise, Collins suggests that companies should focus on one simple thing that they can do better than anyone else.

To find your Hedge Hog, answer these three questions:

1. What are we passionate about?

2. What are we the best at in the world?

3. What drives our economic engine?

Don't create a Hedge Hog in a vacuum, recruit your key team members to collaborate and develop it with you. Then once you have the answers create a simple Ven diagram like the one below that encapsulates what you have discussed and agreed upon. This simple diagram can help you and your team make better decisions.

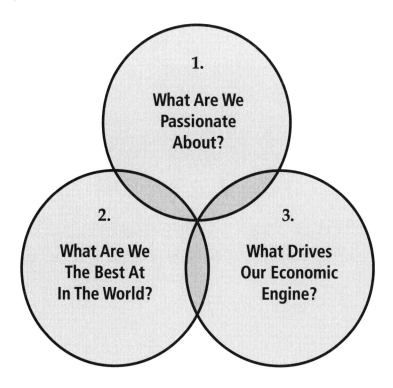

Just Do This

My advice is that you begin by developing your Client Attraction Story. As soon as you have developed your story, jump in and start using it. Over time you will become very comfortable telling it. That's when it's time to work on your attraction conversation. By inserting this story into as many of your conversations as possible, you will attract more clients.

Next, focus on your Power Questions. Use the ones in this book or develop a new set of your own, but create five Power Questions that you can interject into your conversations with your clients.

Finally, use one of the idea generating techniques such as Six Thinking Hats or Observe the Real World to create solutions that not only thrill you and the client, but make you proud. Then stand back and watch as your Authentic Enthusiasm takes hold of you every time you speak about what you do.

If you recall, I started this book by telling my story about landing in the freshly planted soybean field in Hanover

County, Virginia. Allow me to tell the rest of the story. Here's how we came up with the idea to get the stranded plane out of the field.

Mechanicsville LOCAL

JUNE 3, 1986 — "*Stops at every house in town.*" — CIRCULATION 11,035

, board approves

was the old landing in the farmer's field trick
t Saturday when William Whitley and his wife Lee
ne were making the final turn in their approach
Hanover Airport about 6:30 p.m. and their engine
it. The field was freshly cultivated and smooth,
d the powerless landing resulted in no injuries or
nificant damage to the plane. State troopers, Sher-
'e deputies, and first aid and fire volunteers scrambled
initial reports of a plane crash, but it turned out
e field next to Ashcake Road wasn't much different to
d on than the grassy field the Whitleys fly out
at their home in Charlotte, North Carolina.

I Leave You with a Diamond

So much for being hailed as a hero. LeeAnne showed up to the party late and I never made it at all. The police, the FAA and Hanover County Municipal Airport all needed a report. Then there was the dreaded task of calling the owner of the plane to tell him about the unfortunate incident involving his aircraft. The good news was that there were no injuries and the plane was fine. The bad news was that it was sitting in a freshly planted soybean field in Hanover County Virginia.

The next morning the owner of the plane flew up from Charlotte and met us in the field. He was going to attempt a soft field take off. To make the plane as light as possible we removed everything in it that wasn't bolted down. We even drained the fuel, leaving just enough to make it back to the runway. The owner gave it full throttle, pulling back on the yoke so that the nose of the plane would lift up allowing him to take off on the two back wheels. Each time he tried, the nose would go up, but would gradually come back down because the pilot could not build up enough speed in the field.

"Ain't nothin gonna grow there now"

After the third attempt, I looked over at the farmer who owned the soybean field and asked, "Mr. Orock, I've pretty much bought this part of your farm, correct?" Mr. Orock replied, "Yes sir, it's all yours son, there ain't nothin' gonna grow there now." Then I said, "I have a pickup truck that I borrowed from the folks I'm staying with. Would you mind if I drove it up and down in the field to make a little road?" Mr. Orock not only agreed that my idea was a good one, he offered to help. Within minutes we had a caravan of pickup trucks and station wagons driving up and down in the field making a hard packed road. This time when the owner of the plane gave it full throttle and the plane took off!

My wife and I joined him at Hanover County Airport and he let me fly left seat (the pilot in charge sits in the left seat) back to Charlotte. At one point during the flight he looked over at me and said, "You're idea to make a road in the field was worth about $20,000." He went on to explain that if he had not been able to fly the plane out of that field the only alternative would have been to bring in a flat bed truck with a crane and de-wing the airplane. That and the cost of re-winging the plane would have cost me about $15,000. Not to mention that when you're forced to de-wing a plane, it is considered a crash landing and devalues the plane by as much as $5,000. I not only saved our lives, I saved about $20,000.

The lesson I walked away with after making a road in that field is that the ideas you can implement immediately are like diamonds. Imagine coming up with a simple plan that you could implement this afternoon that would change your business, attract a client or add more value. Those simple, yet powerful ideas are diamonds. My goal throughout this book has been to offer you diamonds that are easy to create and implement. My hope is that the lessons you've learned in this book will be as valuable to you as they have been to me.

My Personal Philosophy

In closing I would like to share my personal philosophy for attracting and engaging clients.

1. If you know how to open, you don't have to close. The most powerful way to open is a well-crafted Client Attraction Story.

2. Your questions say more about you than anything else you say. Your ability to listen, understand and synthesize will immediately establish you as a valuable resource.

3. If you believe in what you sell, you're no longer selling, you're just helping. And that's the most powerful position in sales.

These three simple truths have allowed me to grow my businesses and achieve my dreams. I wish the same for you.

Good luck! I look forward to hearing from you.

Bill Whitley
bill@billwhitley.com